ROUTLEDGE LIBRARY EDITIONS:
PHILOSOPHY OF RELIGION

# RELIGION AND THEISM

# RELIGION AND THEISM

The Forwood Lectures delivered at Liverpool University, 1933.

Together with a chapter on the psychological accounts of the origin of belief in God

CLEMENT C. J. WEBB

Volume 38

Routledge
Taylor & Francis Group
LONDON AND NEW YORK

First published in 1934 by Clement C. J. Webb

This edition first published in 2013
by Routledge
2 Park Square, Milton Park, Abingdon, Oxfordshire OX14 4RN

Simultaneously published in the USA and Canada
by Routledge
711 Third Avenue, New York, NY 10017

First issued in paperback 2016

*Routledge is an imprint of the Taylor & Francis Group, an informa business*



*British Library Cataloguing in Publication Data*
A catalogue record for this book is available from the British Library

ISBN: 978-0-415-65969-7 (Set)
ISBN 13: 978-1-138-98498-1 (pbk)
ISBN 13: 978-0-415-82232-9 (hbk)

**Publisher's Note**
The publisher has gone to great lengths to ensure the quality of this reprint but points out that some imperfections in the original copies may be apparent.

**Disclaimer**
The publisher has made every effort to trace copyright holders and would welcome correspondence from those they have been unable to trace.

# RELIGION AND THEISM

THE FORWOOD LECTURES DELIVERED AT LIVERPOOL UNIVERSITY, 1933

TOGETHER WITH A CHAPTER ON

THE PSYCHOLOGICAL ACCOUNTS OF THE ORIGIN OF BELIEF IN GOD

*by*

CLEMENT C. J. WEBB, F.B.A.

*Honorary Fellow of Oriel College, Oxford, and sometime Oriel Professor of the Philosophy of the Christian Religion*

LONDON

GEORGE ALLEN & UNWIN LTD

MUSEUM STREET

FIRST PUBLISHED IN 1934



PRINTED IN GREAT BRITAIN BY
UNWIN BROTHERS LTD., WOKING

# PREFACE

The present volume contains four lectures delivered in February 1933 before the University of Liverpool on the Forwood foundation for lectures on the Philosophy of Religion. To these are added a discussion of the psychological account of the origin of belief in God, with special reference to the theories of Professor Leuba and of Dr. Freud. In writing this I have been much indebted to the references given in Dr. Grensted's Bampton Lectures on *Psychology and God*; and I do not think that I have, in my criticism of Leuba and Freud, added in principle anything to what has already been said about these thinkers in those Bampton Lectures and in Dr. Selbie's Wilde Lectures on *The Psychology of Religion*.

CLEMENT C. J. WEBB

Marston, Oxford
1933

# CONTENTS


| CHAPTER | | PAGE |
|---|---|---|
| I. | THE NOTION OF RELIGION AND THE IDEA OF GOD | 9 |
| II. | RELIGION WITHOUT THEISM<br>A. NATURALISM | 32 |
| III. | RELIGION WITHOUT THEISM<br>B. HUMANISM | 59 |
| IV. | PSYCHOLOGICAL ACCOUNTS OF THE ORIGIN OF BELIEF IN GOD | 87 |
| V. | A VINDICATION OF THEISM | 130 |
| | INDEX | 159 |

# RELIGION AND THEISM

## I

## THE NOTION OF RELIGION AND THE IDEA OF GOD

*Une religion sans Dieu! Mon Dieu, quelle religion!* So, wittily enough, according to a disappointed advocate of the Religion of Humanity inaugurated by Auguste Comte, did the French public of fifty years or so ago respond to the challenge of that system of worship—little in evidence nowadays—wherein the attempt was made to accommodate the traditional piety of Catholic France to the framework of an atheistic philosophy based upon natural science. It is true that Positivism, as an organized religion, cannot be said to have succeeded in replacing or even in effectively competing with those older creeds which do not pretend to confine their attention to what the Positivists called "phenomena." Nevertheless, it may be fairly regarded as the pioneer of a movement which is very much in evidence among us at the present time, and which has made the phrase *Une religion sans Dieu* sound less absurd and paradoxical in the ears of a considerable number of thoughtful people than it presumably did to the generality of those to whom the disciples of Comte addressed themselves in the second half of the nineteenth century.

For we are now familiar with the thought that many of the advantages commonly admitted to attach to what may be called the religious attitude towards life —such as the sense of an ultimate harmony between the aspirations of the individual and the fundamental character of the larger whole whereof he finds himself a part—can be secured without committing oneself to the affirmation of a belief in the existence of a Being describable, in terms drawn from social relations, as King or Lawgiver, Lord or Father, a belief which nothing in the facts ascertained by the natural sciences seems to suggest, while much in the view of the world to which these facts point appears to render it highly improbable.

Such a movement as is indicated by the prevalence of this thought in quarters where not so very long ago it would have been regarded as startling, or even as self-contradictory, plainly implies a possibility of separating the notion of Religion from the idea of God; and, in one form or another, this separation is, as I have said, quite familiar to the minds of thoughtful people to-day. We find respect and even reverence for the great representatives of Religion in the past, recognition that the temper and behaviour exhibited in their lives and teachings are precious things with which humanity cannot, without grave loss, dispense. We find tolerance—or even sometimes warm appreciation—of institutions, ritual or social, which the religion of the past has bequeathed to the present generation. More generally still, we find delight in the works of religious imagination created by the genius of poets, painters, sculptors, architects, musicians, who drew their inspiration from the historical religions. All these sentiments are common enough to-day among people to whom none the less what is usually meant by Theism appears wholly incredible. To such persons belief in the existence of a Being in whose image man was made, on whom the universe explored by the natural sciences depends, and whom we, as his creatures, are called upon to fear, worship, or love, presents itself as no less out of the question for themselves than would be belief in the actual existence of Apollo or the Muse, of John Bull or Uncle Sam, of Father Christmas or the Clerk of the Weather. In the minds of those of whom I am speaking, then, the notion of Religion and the idea of God are not only distinguished, but dissociated; and we find them sometimes apt to speak with a certain contempt of Theism, as a view the maintenance of which by a thoroughly educated man of our day implies not merely a lack of intellectual penetration, but a defective capacity for genuine Religion.

It is to the examination of this supposed irrelevance of Theism to Religion that I propose to devote these Lectures; and it is natural to begin this examination with an attempt to answer the question: What is the true relation between the notion of Religion and the idea of God?

I believe that it would be as vain to demand a formal definition of Religion at the outset of our enquiry as it would be to demand a formal definition of Beauty at the outset of an investigation of an aesthetic problem. None such can be given which would explain to anyone altogether without experience of either what we mean by it; and probably none which could not immediately be countered by an admitted instance of Religion or of Beauty which obviously did not conform to our definition. Nevertheless, I am far from thinking that a consideration of instances in which the presence of Religion or of Beauty is or has been recognized will not help us to understand better than we did before what we and others mean when we use these words.

I do not of course propose in this Lecture to undertake anything like an exhaustive survey of instances —even of those within the narrow range of my own knowledge—in which the presence of Religion is or has been recognized. It must suffice, in the first place, to call attention to some in which there seems to be no reference to the existence of a divine being or beings, and, in the second place, to suggest certain features which, it may plausibly be contended, are exhibited alike by those which do, and by those which do not, imply the existence of such.

Even, if for the moment we do not discriminate between "God" and "gods," and allow the title of "gods" to spirits and ghosts whose right to it might reasonably be disputed, we have to take account of the important fact that one of the two historical religions which claim the greatest number of nominal adherents is Buddhism. Now Buddhism, while it has never denied the real existence of beings whom others than Buddhists worshipped as gods, has often in practice engaged its own followers in the veneration of such beings, and has moreover in the course of its history sometimes developed a genuine theism, yet, perhaps in its original form, certainly in some of its most characteristic phases, has cultivated a spirit and attitude to which it would be very difficult to deny the name "religious," apart from any belief in a God or gods essentially superior to oneself, the object of the religious man's devotion, and the source of his ability to compass the salvation from sin and sorrow which he is seeking. Nor must we forget that the predominant religion of China has been Confucianism, and that Confucius did not claim divinity for himself, nor come forward as a messenger from God, and that he actually discouraged his disciples, even while conforming to established ritual, from occupying their minds with speculations about the beings whom that ritual was intended to propitiate, or indeed about any world or life beyond this. Again, although we may be amply justified by historical precedent in using the word "God," as Spinoza and other philosophers both before him and since him have done, of the ultimate Reality, where there is no thought of reciprocal communion between our spirits and a higher Spirit, and perhaps no certainty that there are any higher spirits than ours possessing a personal or individual mode of existence, such a doctrine of God is not what is commonly understood by Theism. Nevertheless, it may be held with an emotional fervour, and may beget a sense of the seriousness and dignity of life which we cannot reasonably refuse to call religious.

Thus it is clear that instances of Religion can be

found which would be generally admitted to be such, yet, if so, are instances of *religion sans Dieu*, either because no belief in any being describable as "God" is associated with them; or because it is not in the implication of a reference to such a being that the claim to be an instance of Religion consists; or because, although this claim be connected with reference to a being described as God, this being is not "God" in the sense in which Theism may be defined as the doctrine that there is a God.

I will now hazard the suggestion that there are two features which may be found in all instances which would be generally admitted to be instances of Religion; and I will name them provisionally as *ultimacy* and *intimacy*. But it is to be borne in mind that these names are chosen as the result of what may be called philosophical reflexion upon actions, attitudes, feelings, beliefs, in which those who perform or entertain them may be very far from recognizing the characteristics to which the names in question call attention.

I believe it to be true that it belongs to the essence of Religion, even among those to whom it would be absurd to impute a capacity for abstraction such as is necessary for talking of the universe, *totum quod sumus et in quo sumus*, of our experience as a whole, of ultimate reality, or the like, that men should feel themselves to be, if I may so put it, concerned with the innermost heart of things or (to use an alternative metaphor) with what is at the back of everything; and concerned with this not as something remote and indifferent, but rather as something which disturbs and affects us in the depths of our being. We sometimes speak of men making a religion of their profession or business. We always, I think, mean, in using such an expression, to suggest, on the one hand, that for such men there is nothing of interest beyond their profession or business, and, on the other, that this profession or business is not alien to their most private thoughts and desires.

We have seen grounds for affirming that there may be Religion, with what I have called its *ultimacy* and its *intimacy*, but without the association therewith of belief in a being such as is usually indicated by the word "God," in some kind of intercourse with whom is experienced that consciousness of intimate touch with what is at the back or at the heart of everything which we call religious. Yet it does not follow that the idea of God can in the same way be dissociated from an experience of this kind. There may indeed be brought forward some arguments in favour of such a possible dissociation. It cannot be denied that both in the speculations of philosophers and in the practice of ordinary men in times or places wherein the existence of a God or gods is commonly assumed as beyond reasonable doubt, belief in a being or beings to whom the name is applicable may coexist with an absence of the feelings, attitudes, or behaviour which we should call religious. Men have thought proofs of God's existence irrefutable, or have never dreamed of doubting that he existed, whom yet no one would describe as religious men. But I think it may be shown that the use of the word "God" by philosophers for the first Cause, or all-comprehending Whole, or ultimate Reality, is an inheritance from a religious tradition, and therefore misleading, so far as its employment to denote an object which could be apprehended apart from any specifically religious experience inevitably carries with it irrelevant associations of a religious kind. It was, I believe, the immensely important contribution made to the understanding of Religion by Kant's attack on the scholastic proofs of God's existence in combination with his assertion that God was postulated by our moral consciousness, that he thereby established the essential connexion of the idea of God with an experience not merely theoretical. The circumstance that he insufficiently discriminated Religion from Morality does not impair the value of his insistence on the inadequacy of what he called "pure reason" to remove Theism from the sphere of religious faith to that of scientific knowledge.

On the case of men who have never thought of denying the existence of God, yet are not religious, I would make two observations. The first is that we have here an instance of a familiar phenomenon, that of reliance on unverified and uncriticized authority; and that the belief thus accepted at second hand would never have been originally acquired without a precedent religious experience. The second observation I would make is that its reception on authority by the men of whom we are speaking was unquestionably aided by the secret presence in their souls of an undeveloped capacity for religious experience, such a capacity being in truth a normal feature of human nature.

We thus seem to have reached a somewhat unsatisfactory result. The notion of Religion does not, it would seem, imply the idea of God; yet the idea of God implies the notion of Religion, since it is the idea of a Being of whose existence we could only become aware through an experience of a sort which would fall under the notion of Religion. It would seem at any rate to be demanded of us by this situation that we should be able to state an intelligible ground of distinction between a religious experience which *is* and one which *is not* an experience of God; and, so far at any rate, we have come upon nothing which would help us to do this. We may therefore not unreasonably suspect that, while we have not been wholly wasting our time, since, were there no *prima facie* case for a *religion sans Dieu*, much popular contemporary thought and talk about religion would be inexplicable, a closer examination might reveal an intimate connexion, or even a correlation, between the idea of God and the notion of Religion; and might show that the apparent absence of such a correlation is to be accounted for by ambiguities in the language employed in the discussion of the problem. We shall therefore find it advisable to make a fresh start.

Of these two words, *Religion* and *God*, it is plain that the former is what we may call a *subjective*, the latter what we may call an *objective* term. For the former designates a state or attitude of mind or, at least, a kind of behaviour which is found in human beings under certain circumstances; the latter an object, real or imaginary, the actual or supposed presence of which excites that state of mind or occasions that kind of behaviour in human beings. Thus described, the notion of Religion may seem, from the point of view often adopted by psychologists, to be prior to the idea of God, inasmuch as it is the notion of a fact of consciousness of which we may be directly or immediately aware; while the idea of God may be regarded as resulting from an act of inference from this fact of consciousness to a cause beyond and independent of the consciousness in which it occurs; and this would harmonize with the opinion that belief in God is no necessary part of the experience of Religion. On the other hand, the legitimacy of this psychological point of view may itself be called in question. It may be pointed out that consciousness is essentially consciousness of an object, and that this object, whether or no in the last resort independent of the mind which apprehends it, is at any rate distinct from the act of consciousness in which it is apprehended; and that it is a fallacy to suppose that only by way of a causal inference from its own immediately apprehended states does the mind become aware of an object distinct from itself.

In any case, whether or no this criticism be justified—as I think myself that it is—it can hardly be questioned that, historically considered, reflexion on objects apprehended precedes reflexion on our apprehension of them. In general philosophy, the study of reality taken as known precedes enquiry into the nature of knowledge itself, although that may afterwards come to be considered as a prerequisite of the investigation of the objects of knowledge. So too in the philosophy of Religion, interest in the nature of God, the object of religious reverence, precedes interest in our experience of feeling or paying such reverence; and the idea of God may thus be called prior to the notion of Religion in the sense that men think about God before they think about their own thought about him, and indeed could not think about the latter if it were not there to be thought about; that is, if they had not already thought about God.

But it may be said that I am now assuming the very point which is in dispute. For, if Religion is essentially the apprehension of God, and is there related to God as subject to object, it must be impossible to entertain a notion of Religion which does not at once involve, as its inseparable correlative, the idea of God.

Now I do indeed think that, when taken in their widest application, "Religion" and "God" are correlative terms; but it is none the less true that, as actually used, they are not always so. For either may be employed in a restricted sense, in which it is only correlative to the other if that also be made subject to a corresponding restriction. As a matter of fact, "Religion" is frequently used in the widest possible sense for states or attitudes of mind or kinds of behaviour which are felt to have in common a certain quality, perhaps not susceptible of a definition which would explain its nature to anyone with no personal experience of it, but easily to be recognized by those who have such an experience. The word "God," on the other hand, may be understood, not as the designation of the object of religious reverence, whatever that object may really be, and however it may be imaginatively represented, but only of that object as represented in a particular way, which can easily be shown to be but one among many in which it has been envisaged during the long and diversified history of man's quest of or commerce with—and perhaps, as Pascal has taught us, the quest implies the commerce —that which ever haunts the human soul as a Presence at once all-embracing and infinite, to lay hold whereof would be to discover the meaning of all our experience and of the existence of the world wherein we find ourselves.

The particular way of envisaging the object of Religion which is thus nowadays specially associated with the name "God" is what is usually meant by the word "Theism." This term and the corresponding term "Theist" are of no great antiquity, and were doubtless formed—in the seventeenth century—to designate the opposite of "Atheism" and "Atheist," without the implication, which had become associated with the somewhat earlier expressions "Deism" and

"Deist," of indifference or hostility to the belief in a special revelation of God over and above that made to all men alike in the fabric of nature and the constitution of our faculties. The terms "Atheism" and "Atheist" themselves, though negative in form, are far more ancient than their seeming positives; and it is doubtful whether they were originally intended to signify the contrary of that which "Theism" is commonly understood to mean. Even etymologically[1] there are grounds for holding that by ἄθεος the Greeks meant not one who denied that there were gods, but rather one who did not concern himself with θεῖα (or, as we should say, with religion), *parcus deorum cultor et infrequens*; and unquestionably the name of "atheist" has throughout the ages been applied to persons who notoriously did *not* deny that there existed any being entitled to be called "God." When the martyr Polycarp[2] was called upon by his pagan persecutors to cry "Away with the atheists" in repudiation of his Christian brethren, and replied by looking sternly upon the hostile multitude and uttering the desired exclamation in reference not to the Christians but to them, certainly neither did they suppose him, nor he suppose them, to deny the existence of any being who could be called God. But

[1] I owe this observation to Professor J. A. Smith.

[2] Eusebius, *Hist. Eccl.* iv. 15.

they did hold him guilty of *impiety* in his neglect of the worship of the gods acknowledged by the State; and he them of no less *impiety* in their worship of those gods instead of that One God to whom alone was in his eyes due the service which they diverted to others. The very Epicureans who were regarded in antiquity as the champions of Atheism in philosophy were far from denying the existence of gods. It was matter of common knowledge that they believed the forms of superhuman beauty and majesty which had inspired the imagination of artists and poets to have been actually presented to the senses of men in sleep, having floated off from real beings inhabiting remote regions of the universe. But they denied that these beings concerned themselves with human affairs, or heeded the worship which was paid to them by those whom the chance encounter with their wandering images had stricken with an admiration only to be expressed by such tokens of reverence. Even at the very period in which the word "Theism" first appears, the man who was esteemed the prince of atheists was one who spoke of God on every page of his chief work, and for whom the highest of human activities was the *amor intellectualis Dei*. Yet, because, holding as he did that we should not seek to be loved by God in return, he seemed to empty of meaning the prayer and worship by which men sought to commend themselves to God and to win his favour, Spinoza was reckoned *impious*, as denying to God what most of his contemporaries believed him to require at our hands. *Impiety*, not the speculative denial that any God or gods exist, is the historical significance of "Atheism"; and thus the use of "Theism" as its opposite is really a misfit and due to a misunderstanding.

This excursion into lexicography is not of merely philological interest; for in the light of it we shall find it less difficult to answer the question whether Religion and Theism imply one another. The truth seems to be that "Atheism" in its historical sense is the negation of Religion, but that "Theism" has been employed, in accordance with the prevalent mode of thought at the time when the word came into use—a mode of thought which should not have survived the criticism of Kant—to denote (or at least to include) a doctrine of God's existence based upon grounds which, as stated, abstract from any such specifically religious experience as alone gives its peculiar significance to the word "God." The attempt to deduce the reasonableness of Religion from a belief in God's existence based on other than religious grounds is bound to fail; for the non-religious arguments alleged in support of the belief can only help to establish a genuinely religious faith when they are themselves interpreted in the light of that religious experience which alone originally makes us aware of God at all. Apart from this they cannot reveal God to us; they can at the most remove obstacles to the reception by our minds of a revelation mediated by that capacity for communion with the divine which is, as I said above, a normal feature of our humanity.[1]

But not only has "Theism" thus come to suggest a use of the word "God" by philosophical writers in which its proper relation to religious experience is forgotten; it has also tended to be associated in the minds of many of those who repudiate it with a certain way of envisaging the object of Religion which, as was made abundantly evident in the earlier part of this Lecture, is by no means the only way in which it can be and has been envisaged.

[1] I insist, though only in passing, upon this normality of Religion, because it is sometimes supposed that to hold a specifically religious experience to be necessary to religious faith is to restrict Religion to a few exceptional persons, prophets and saints and mystics. But this no more follows from the premises than it follows, because, apart from a capacity to appreciate beauty of sound, it would be impossible to make men musical by mathematical demonstrations even of propositions of special interest to students of musical theory, therefore the power of enjoying some kind of music is not common among human beings of every grade of intelligence and culture.

To the imagination of a child, assisted, it may be, by that of Renaissance painters who assimilated the Christian God to the Jupiter of the classical poets, the word "God" may call up the picture of an old man with a beard seated on the clouds or on a throne beyond the sky. Writers in the popular press appear sometimes to suppose that this is the kind of God in whom those believe who are content to use traditional language about the law, the wrath, or the judgment of God, language which seems to them to convey important truth for which no other or better expression has yet been found. But men of deeper insight than these journalistic critics have found a stumbling-block in representations of that which they are called upon to worship under the guise of a supernatural authority, external to themselves. Such representations Blake caricatured in his "old Nobodaddy," and Wordsworth dismissed as irrelevant to his deeper religious experience when he wrote:

> All strength, all terror, single or in bands,
> That ever was put forth in personal form,
> Jehovah with his thunders and the choirs
> Of shouting Angels and the empyreal thrones,
> —I pass them unalarmed.

And not a few thinkers in recent times, who have been far from denying the supreme value of Religion as a revelation of what is best and highest in the universe have yet thought that the evidence to hand does not warrant us in supposing a Being to exist therein, with whom we can enter into relations describable in terms appropriate to our social intercourse with our fellows, yet possessing the perfection which might seem to belong only to the all-inclusive Reality or Absolute. And not only so, but it has also been held that such a supposition must subjugate the freedom and depress the dignity of the finite personality which otherwise would find nothing in the universe higher than those activities of its own conscious mind wherein that universe, after the age-long travail of its evolution,

> Beholds itself, and knows itself divine.

The two Lectures which follow this will be devoted to the consideration of attempts to find scope for the religious capacities of our nature without involving us in the acceptance of a conception of the object of Religion which should be liable to such criticism as that of which I have just been sketching the outline. Those who make these attempts may be discriminated into two classes. With one of these the main objection to "Theism" is its inconsistency with the view of the world suggested by the natural sciences, with its unimaginable vastness of extension in space and duration in time, and its obvious indifference to our desires and ideals; and with the insignificance in this view of our whole race as a transient phenomenon on a relatively infinitesimal portion of the universe. With the other class, what is emphasized is rather the spiritual greatness which belongs to that very humanity which the former line of thought depreciated, in that it has achieved an autonomous personality, claiming for its own intuitions such independence of any dictation by external authority as is inconsistent with the acknowledgment of a divine Lord whose word must be unquestionably obeyed, and whose infinite perfection must leave to his creatures no scope for a truly creative originality.

It may indeed strike us as paradoxical that the dissociation of Religion from Theism should be due to two such mutually opposite considerations as that of the littleness of man in the physical universe and that of his greatness in the moral; and even more so that the two considerations may sometimes be found combined in an assault on the anthropomorphism which is imputed to the conception of the object of Religion associated by many with the word "God." But the problem at issue in both cases is that of the position of personality in the universe; whether, as it appears in us finite beings, it is the only thing of its kind therein; or whether it can be attributed to the ultimate Reality, of which all that we or any other beings capable of experiencing can ever experience is a part or an expression. In considering such finite personality as ours we may either dwell upon its apparently brief span of existence and its feeble control of its environment, in contrast with the magnitude of the periods which preceded its appearance and may follow its extinction, and of the forces which environ its existence; or, on the other hand, upon the unique dignity of that which knows and values, the "thinking reed" of Pascal, in a world otherwise without self-consciousness, however overwhelming its size and dateless its duration. Whichever we insist upon, we may be disposed to think that belief in a Personality belonging to or controlling the universe is incongruous alike with the fact that the only personality whose existence is indubitable seems to be intimately associated with bodily phenomena of a rare and peculiar kind, and not with those exhibited throughout the range of our scientific observation of the material world; and with the claim of personality where it does exist, to an initiative and autonomy which it could hardly possess in the presence of a personality or personalities already in complete and permanent control of the whole environment in the manipulation whereof ours has its sole means of self-expression.

It will be my purpose in the concluding Lecture of this course to suggest reasons for holding that the attempts made to dissociate Religion from Theism which these contrasted considerations conspire to instigate are unsatisfactory; and that the object of Religion may be conceived in such a way as to justify much in traditional language and practice which the opponents of "Theism" are bound to reject; while at the same time neither contradicting the legitimate demands of natural science, nor yet impairing the moral dignity of finite personality.

# II

# RELIGION WITHOUT THEISM

## A. NATURALISM

I HAVE called the subject of this Lecture "Religion without Theism (Naturalism)," and that of my third Lecture as "Religion without Theism (Humanism)." The distinction intended is one which I indicated at the end of my first Lecture, when pointing out that those who, while accepting Religion as an element of high importance in human life, would dissociate it from Theism, do this on one of two grounds. Either they find an incongruity between the belief that the universe is governed by a spiritual being conceived after the analogy of a human person and the knowledge which we derive from the investigations of the natural sciences of the extent and duration of the universe and of the evolution of life and consciousness therein; or else they consider the autonomy and freedom from external dictation claimed by the human conscience inconsistent with the acknowledgment of any authority transcending that of our own reason, or of any will antecedently determining our activities. Divergent as these two grounds may at first sight seem to be, the former emphasizing the littleness, the latter the greatness of man, they may nevertheless be combined. Human personality may be regarded as at once, in its aspect as a natural phenomenon, transient and insignificant, and, in its aspect as a spiritual value, the best and highest thing with which we have any acquaintance; and the inference may be drawn from this its twofold character that it neither points, as theists affirm, to the control of nature by a superhuman personality or personalities, nor would win for itself a real increase of value or dignity by the admission that Nature is subject to such a control—but rather the reverse. Though we have thus not to do with two incompatible alternatives, we may nevertheless conveniently distinguish the objection to Theism of which the main motive is a deep impression of our insignificance in the immensity of Nature from that which is inspired by enthusiasm for spiritual independence. In appending to the former the label of Naturalism, it will be observed that I am departing from what is probably now the most common use of this word. For I shall be using it to denote a view which is religious, but not theistic, whereas it is more often employed as the designation of a view which leaves no room for Religion at all, except as an illusion arising at a certain stage of the mental development of conscious organisms. But, as this whole enquiry presupposes that those whom it concerns attribute to Religion a higher status than this, and conceive it to be a permanently valuable element in human life, no ambiguity arising from this cause need introduce any confusion into our treatment of the problem before us.

Now it is undeniable that an emotion of a character which would be universally recognized as religious is called forth in many men by the contemplation of Nature. In the famous saying of Kant with which the concluding section of his *Critique of Practical Reason* begins, and which is inscribed upon his tomb at Königsberg, "the starry heavens above us and the moral law within us," are placed side by side as the two things which fill the human breast with that emotion of awe or reverence which belongs to the very essence of Religion. Moreover, it is certain that Nature does not, as apprehended by our senses, at all resemble the outward forms which invite us to enter into relations of human fellowship. Primitive as is the impulse to "personify," as the phrase goes, natural objects and processes, men have always been conscious of a distinction between their fellow-men and the superhuman beings of whose activities they believed themselves to be witnesses, when noting the apparent movements of the heavenly bodies, of wind and waters, and the rest. When, at a more advanced stage of intellectual development, the mind is more deeply influenced by a sense of the unity of the mighty whole in the midst of which man finds himself, and he is led to divine a Mind directing it and controlling the operations of its parts, which thus tend to lose the appearance of separate beings, each with an individuality like that of a man or woman, the disproportion between the scale on which this world-directing Mind must function and that on which our minds do so, thrusts itself upon the imagination, and we are led to ask, with the Psalmist: "What is man that God should be mindful of him?" At a yet later period the difference between man and God, whether envisaged as the Orderer or as the Soul of the world, becomes yet more evident. We are less and less ready to assume the divine intelligence to be analogous in detail to the human; and at last we become suspicious of any view which lays stress upon such an analogy; and are ready to jettison "theism" in the sense of a theory committed to insistence thereon. Yet, all the time, the sentiment of awe or reverence in the presence of Nature (and I would call attention to this word "presence") may tend to increase with the increased sense of discrepancy between the scale of human actions and of natural happenings. It is not even killed by a growing conviction that Nature is far from exhibiting conformity to our moral standards. Yet it is undoubtedly affected thereby, in consequence of the value set upon these, which, we must remember, constitute, according to Kant's saying, the other chief occasion of religious reverence. Had they constituted, as Kant himself seems often to hold, the *sole* occasion of it, it would be difficult to account for its persistence as directed to an object wholly dissociated from them. But in fact the moral consciousness is *not* the only root of Religion. Primitive men seem to have found no difficulty in worshipping gods whose conduct they did not expect to conform to the moral standards acknowledged in their own communities, to which these gods did not belong; and it was only after long and arduous efforts that prophets and philosophers succeeded in establishing the rule that the moral consciousness has the right to test by its own canons assertions respecting the will and actions of God. With the establishment of this rule there is undoubtedly inaugurated a tendency which, as the progress of natural science reveals ever more decidedly an apparent indifference on the part of Nature to our moral standards, has by our day "ungodded" Nature, if I may use the expression, not only in the sense of denying the existence of an anthropomorphically imagined Director of its course, but even in the sense of discarding the religious reverence with which our forefathers were accustomed to regard it. Nevertheless, the habit of such reverence is too deeply ingrained for it to perish whenever a theoretical justification, which had not been its original motive, has ceased to be acceptable.

A non-theistic religion, inspired by what certain thinkers of last century have called "cosmic emotion," may, however, continue to exist. It will not express itself, like older religions, in prayer and sacrifice; it will not lend itself to the elaboration of a theology; but it may profoundly affect imaginative souls, and utter itself in poetry and art. It is entitled to be called Religion, for it exhibits the two principal marks of Religion which I have noted above. It is directed towards what is taken to be *ultimate*, and it is experienced in an *intimate* sense of kinship with this object and of responsiveness to its appeal. Yet it may very well be found in combination with a *humanistic* religion, drawing its inspiration from the other source recognized by Kant, the consciousness of the moral law within us, but now that the existence of the supposed divine giver of the moral law who was also believed to be the Governor of the universe is rejected for lack of evidence, and also on account of the apparent absence from the course of nature of any regard to the moral law, directing its reference to *Man*, as the sole creator and embodiment of that law. That such a religion can exhibit the mark of *intimacy* is obvious; it is *within* us, as Kant said, that the moral law is to be found; that it can exhibit the mark of what I will venture to call *ultimacy* is plainly far less clear; and we shall see, if we study a religion of this type, that doubt of its capacity to do so is apt to haunt it like a ghost, or (to vary the metaphor) to feed "like a worm i' the bud" upon what, but for this, might have been able to accomplish a victory, such as a New Testament writer claims for his own faith, a "victory that overcometh the world."

I now propose to examine, as an instance of this kind of religion, that expounded in a remarkable book, published a few years ago by Professor Julian Huxley, called *Religion without Revelation*. It is a book interesting as the mirror of a personality attractive for its reverent appreciation of what is best in life, and its gift of vivid self-disclosure unmarred by the distressing egoism which disfigures some other recent autobiographies dealing with religion. It is interesting also as the confession of a distinguished man of science who by descent and upbringing is in close touch with some of the noblest traditions of English life. Lastly, it is interesting as, in many respects, representative of the mind of the generation, now passing into middle life to which its author belongs.

There is one tradition which Professor Huxley's book carries on, and which he, as he reminds us himself, has, as it were, an hereditary right to carry on, that of an intense passion for truth which makes them whom it masters intolerant of any conclusion which even seems to anticipate evidence or to tamper with the scales in which evidence is weighed. This passion was eminently characteristic both of his famous grandfather, Thomas Huxley, who coined the word "agnostic," and of his no less famous ancestor, concerning whose training of his scholars his poet son has written:

> For rigorous teachers seized my youth,
> And purged its faith, and trimmed its fire,
> Showed me the high, white star ot Truth,
> There bade me gaze, and there aspire.[1]

In this respect moreover—and not only in this respect—Professor Huxley's work recalls the writings of that brilliant and prematurely lost thinker of an earlier generation, William Kingdon Clifford; but there is a point of contrast between them to which it is relevant to the purpose of this Lecture to call attention.

[1] Matthew Arnold, *Stanzas from the Grande Chartreuse.*

Clifford and Professor Huxley alike stand for the possibility of an attitude towards life which may properly be described as religious, yet is divorced altogether from Theism. But Clifford, who was brought up to believe in the Christian God, and was, as a young man, a devout Churchman, frankly allows[1] "that theistic belief is a comfort or a solace to those who hold it, and that the loss of it is a very painful loss." "We," he goes on, speaking for those who, like himself, had undergone that loss, "have seen the spring sun shine out of an empty heaven to light up a soulless earth. We have felt with utter loneliness that the Great Companion is dead. Our children," he continues, "it may be hoped, will know that sorrow only by the reflex light of a wondering compassion." Professor Julian Huxley, on the other hand, who, although he was, as he tells us, introduced in childhood by "very simple prayers" to "the mysterious word *God*," received little or no teaching of the kind commonly called religious (what he did receive being "wholly unorthodox in quality" and "extremely small in quantity"), "had no picture of the "something, call it a power if you like," to which the name *God* was applied, "which came in contact with my life by being responsible for such external phenomena as the weather"—"had no

[1] *Lectures and Essays*, p. 389.

picture" of it, "no belief that it was personal." Thus he was able to fulfil Clifford's hope for his posterity by escaping in his own person any such sorrow for the loss of a Great Companion as Clifford himself experienced. Yet he has been by no means a stranger to many of those spiritual struggles, miseries, and satisfactions of which religious biographies are full; and the circumstance that he is well acquainted with these as phenomena of his own inner life, while unconscious of entertaining any thought of God as "personal," has been for him a convincing demonstration that Theism is not essential to Religion.[1]

Professor Huxley's book is called *Religion without Revelation*, but its contents do not correspond very accurately with its title, unless "revelation" be taken in a very narrowly restricted sense, to which indeed the author has not always, when off his guard, in fact confined his own use of the word. I shall attempt in my following remarks to show (1) that Professor Huxley's own account of religious experience rather suggests a theistic background than is intrinsically inconsistent with it; (2) that his contrary belief is based upon a misapprehension of what is meant by Theism as a philosophical theory; and (3) that the "Humanism," as we may call it—although Professor Huxley does not

[1] *Religion without Revelation*, pp. 106–8.

use the word, and although his objections to Theism are based rather upon its supposed incongruity with our knowledge of Nature than upon its alleged incompatibility with the dignity of Man—this Humanism, which is implied in his own alternative theory of the nature of religious experience, is itself by no means easily reconcilable either with his own account of that experience, or with his general philosophical position.

The theme of Professor Huxley's book is that Religion may and does exist where there is no belief in a revelation from without, or a God who should make such a revelation: that its phenomena may be sufficiently explained as products of the human mind itself under the influence of its natural environment; and that it is not on this account to be treated as a vain and illusory thing, but rather as, like the beauty created by human art, possessing the highest value for those whose lives are enriched and ennobled thereby.

What he describes as "the idea of God as a supernatural being," which appears to him in retrospect never to have been to himself more than a suggestion from without, verified by nothing in his own experience, "religious" though it often was, he has definitely rejected, he informs us, with an "enormous sense of spiritual relief."[1] This confession invites us to consider the question how far his attempt to show that the idea of God—I will not say at this stage "as a supernatural being," because I believe this expression to carry with it, for Professor Huxley, implications which are not, to my own mind, necessarily involved in Theism—that the idea of God as a Being at the least not less real than ourselves, from whom we can distinguish ourselves, and to whom prayer and thanksgiving can be reasonably addressed, is an appendage to Religion, whereof it may rid itself to its own great advantage.

I have observed that, notwithstanding Professor Huxley's assertions to the contrary, his own religious experience, as described by himself, suggests a theistic background. The very word "revelation," used in his title to designate the theistic explanation of that experience, occurs when he is, I think, for the moment off his guard. For we find him saying that "the statement that moral *revelations* or mystic visions are the result of communication by personal, supernatural beings is merely one way, and an erroneous way, of interpreting the undoubted facts."[2] It is true, indeed, that the description of certain of these "facts" as strictly "revelations" is intended to be part of the

[1] Page 53. [2] Page 136.

erroneous interpretation of the facts which he is repudiating; but this is not the natural way of taking the language employed; and elsewhere, though the word "revelation" is not found, we read of "reverence" as "a way in which the mind shall walk if it is to achieve things worth achieving."[1] We cannot but ask, "Reverence to whom?" For that, as Kant has pointed out, "reverence" implies a personal object, seems plain. From some passages, however, one would be led to infer that for Professor Huxley the Universe is the object towards which this desirable or even necessary attitude of reverence is directed. Yet it is clear that he does not regard the Universe as itself personal, or as the expression of a superhuman personality. We learn indeed that the very unity in virtue of which "Nature's chaos" (the phrase is his) is envisaged as a *universe* at all is imposed upon it (not, it would seem, merely discovered in it) by the human mind. Yet, apart from this unity, it cannot surely be an object of reverence at all. But perhaps Professor Huxley would admit all this. For he expressly likens the unification of "Nature's chaos" by the human mind to the activity of the human mind in the creation of works of art; and we doubtless do feel an emotion of reverence for great poetry, painting, or music, which we reckon as

[1] Page 361.

productions of the human mind; which, however, it is to be remembered, though, not, in abstraction from their creators, themselves persons, are yet always the works of persons who therein express their personality. But, even so, our difficulties are not at an end. For Professor Huxley in one place dogmatically lays it down[1] that all reality consists of "events, which are all events in the history of a single substance," which, "looked at from outside are matter, experienced from inside are mind." Here he seems to have forgotten that he has made the unity of the world a creation of the human mind, and to have fallen back into a position resembling that of Spinoza, who assuredly did not regard the Single Substance which he called indifferently God or Nature as indebted to the human mind for its unity. It is not, I think, unfair to point this out, as indicating the difficulty experienced by our authors in consistently maintaining a view so alien to the instinctive tendencies of our mind as that which supposes that we put into Nature the only unity which it possesses. But, even if we forget this divagation (or at least postpone its consideration till we reach the third head of our criticism), and if we make the fullest possible allowance for the consideration that theistic beliefs have so far prevailed in the

[1] Page 76.

past as to colour the only language available for the description of facts patient of quite another than a theistic interpretation, we must nevertheless, I think, admit that what Professor Huxley calls "*facts* of the spiritual life,"[1] and enumerates as "the conviction of sin, the desire of righteousness, the sense of absolution, the peace of communion," are, if not necessarily, at least more naturally envisaged with a theistic background, in which there is a righteous God, against whom we have sinned, from whom we seek forgiveness, in reconciliation with whom we find our peace, than with the background of a chaotic Nature which owes whatever unity it possesses to the "organising power of the human mind." [2]

That it appears otherwise to Professor Huxley is, I believe, largely due to his identification of Theism with a doctrine of God far cruder and more onesidedly "transcendent" (as the phrase goes) than that of, for example, the classical theology of Christendom. I cannot help thinking that he fails to realize how little "anthropomorphic," in the popular acceptation of that term, is the theology of such thinkers as St. Augustine or St. Thomas Aquinas, whom yet it would be strange to describe as not being theists. When he speaks of a "supernatural personal being," what I have called the

[1] Page 49. [2] Page 41.

classical theology of Christendom would not indeed repudiate the applicability of the expression to God: but would take it in a sense not incompatible with affirming the immanence of God in Nature, and with avoiding the assertion that "God is *a person*." It would probably surprise many critics of traditional language to learn what is nevertheless true, that "the personality of God" is a phrase unknown to Christian theology until well within the last two hundred years; that "personality" was not reckoned among the divine "attributes" so-called, and was long ascribed to God only in connexion with the "three persons" worshipped by the Christian Church as one God; and that even the early Socinian divines were not concerned to insist upon ascribing "personality" to him, but only to contend that, *if* the term were employed in reference to God (which employment they were inclined to deprecate), he would be spoken of as *One* Person and not as three. I do not wish now to pursue further this history, on which I have dwelt at length elsewhere[1]: but it is, I think, relevant to my present subject to point out that to define Theism as the doctrine of a "supernatural, personal being" is only defensible in a loose and popular sense, and that many qualifications

[1] In my Gifford Lectures on *God and Personality*, Lecture III.

must be introduced if the definition is to be taken as applicable to the doctrine of some of those who would be universally allowed to be among the most influential representatives of a theistic view of the world.

I will defer to my last Lecture a more positive account of what I understand by Theism; but I think I have said enough to support my suggestion that Professor Huxley takes the word "Theism" in a sense narrower than it will reasonably bear. On the other hand, I should fully admit that it is not solely because he takes Theism so that he is bound to reject it. In any form, a genuine Theism is, I think, incompatible with a conception of Man as the highest being within our experience, such as Professor Huxley, in common with the definitely "humanistic" critics of Theism, sometimes seems to entertain. I should not regard any view as entitled to be called Theism which did not involve the reasonableness of a *worshipping* attitude on Man's part, and therefore the reality of a Being within our experience, so far transcending humanity in the scale of values as to justify this attitude.

Whatever be the case, however, with others, Professor Huxley seems to me to set a value upon certain phenomena of the religious life which it is difficult to ascribe to them, except upon a theistic interpretation, such as he thinks can be dispensed with. Such are "the feeling of forgiveness and grace to a soul struggling with the sense of sin, the poignant experience of the value of others' atonement, or of one's own suffering; the sense of communion with and peace in the realities that are around us." Professor Huxley indeed says: "Not only do these remain facts of psychological experience whatever interpretation or explanation of them be offered, but their value is not in the interpretation, but in themselves."[1] But surely, apart from an interpretation which I at any rate should call theistic, their value would be very different from that which, as so interpreted, they would possess; just as the experience of human love may be justly said to have value in itself, independently of any theory we may entertain about it, yet, were we in any instance to discover that the object of this were a mere creature of the lover's imagination, it would seriously affect our estimate of the value of the experience in that case. Even though it be true that the qualities imputed by the lover to the beloved person are often in fact rather imagined by the lover to be in him or her than really present there, and that this circumstance does not render the love valueless; yet I do not think we should so judge if there were not and never had been or would be any being *in rerum natura* possessed of

[1] Page 317.

the qualities thus wrongly imputed. Professor Huxley himself,[1] while he tells us "that he believes that sin exists and the sense of sin," goes on to liken the latter to the measles, which are nothing to be ashamed of, or to be proud of either. But does he really suppose that if we so regard "the sense of sin," it remains a sense of *sin* at all, and not merely something we have called so in ignorance of its true nature? He 'believes,' he tells us again,[2] in grace, not as a gift from divine power, but as a special inner illumination and peace which comes whenever an unexplained, or at least undeserved, moment of spiritual achievement is thrust on the mind. But who or what thrusts it on the mind? And is not the word "undeserved" meaningless except in the context of a world ultimately under moral government? For our author is surely not here speaking of "desert" in relation to our fellows; he has in mind, I take it, not so much the experience of, let us say, gratitude shown to us by some neighbour whom we are not conscious of having gone out of our way to serve, as the experience of what some people would call a "mystical" sense of that which Professor Huxley himself elsewhere describes as "communion with and peace in the realities that surround us." Such a sense undoubtedly does come inexplicably to

[1] Page 365. [2] Page 366.

some persons at some times; but only because we interpret its advent as an occurrence in a morally governed universe is it intelligible to call it "undeserved" rather than "irrational." If we can rightly speak of "the realities that surround us" as something with which we can have "communion," we are surely on the threshold of a theistic interpretation of the world whereof these realities are the part with which we are in contact. Still more evidently is this so if it be true, as I believe it to be, that what is meant by calling God "personal" is ultimately not that we cannot explain the world otherwise for the purposes of natural science than by attributing its origin to a being like one of ourselves; but that our religious experience is experience of a communion, different indeed from the social intercourse which we enjoy with our fellow human beings, yet not merely metaphorically described by terms appropriate to that intercourse, but rather described thus *a fortiori*, that which gives meaning to those terms, the "warmth and intimacy" (to use a phrase employed in a somewhat different connexion by William James) of the response, being present here in a greater rather than in a less measure, as compared with the reciprocal relations of finite spirits.

There are, however, indications that Professor

Huxley's quarrel with Theism is not merely on the ground that it is an unsatisfactory interpretation or explanation of the facts of what we call specifically religious experience. He seems to associate with the theistic interpretation of "grace" what he reckons as an unwarrantable claim on the part of Religion to a monopoly of the kind of "inner illumination and peace," which he understands by that name. "In reality," he tells us,[1] "it operates in every sphere of the mind's life." But surely the theist does not suppose that God does not so operate? Surely he does not think that no good gift comes down from God except those received in that kind of experience which is contrasted with other kinds as "religious"? When Professor Huxley says later on[2] that "to be always religious is as intolerable as to be always laughing, or always playing golf" is he really saying more than the late Baron Friedrich von Hügel—a champion of the theistic interpretation of religious experience if ever there was one—was for ever saying, namely, that it is to the interest of Religion itself to allow their due independence to other activities which belong, no less than Religion itself, to the God-given nature of man?

The Humanistic criticism, as I have called it, which objects to Theism as a disparagement of the dignity

[1] Page 367. [2] Page 374.

of human nature, and which I shall illustrate in my third Lecture of this course, although it sometimes puts in an appearance in Professor Huxley's pages, seems to me, as I have already intimated, incongruous alike with his own account of religious experience and with his general philosophical outlook. As to the former, I have perhaps already sufficiently insisted upon its implication of a superhuman source of inspiration, with which in Religion the human soul finds itself in communion. As to the latter, the passage about reality consisting of events in the history of a single Substance, which as observed from without are matter, as experienced from within are mind, suggests, as I have already taken occasion to point out, a view akin to that of Spinoza, a philosopher whose teaching, for reasons which are not far to seek, has a special attraction for thoughtful men of science. It is no doubt true that Spinoza, though no humanist, was also no theist in the sense in which Professor Huxley rejects Theism, and in which I am here using the word. He speaks continually of God, and the crowning activity of the human mind is for him *amor intellectualis Dei*, a love of God arising from the understanding, partial though it may be, of that wonderful order or system which may be called indifferently Nature or God. But just because he who attains to this love of God does not look that God should love him in return—according to a passage in the *Ethics* which excited the enthusiastic approval of Goethe on account of what seemed to him to be its sublime unselfishness—it cannot be called with any propriety "communion." Yet it is by this very name that Professor Huxley describes the culmination of his own religious experience. I cannot but conclude that to that experience neither Humanism nor Spinozism does in truth provide as congenial a background as does Theism, despite Professor Huxley's own leanings now to Humanism, now to Spinozism, and his emphatic rejection of Theism.

Nevertheless, I am very far from denying that there is something which may well appear incongruous, and, if I may so express myself, out of scale in the suggestion which Theism may seem to involve, that behind that universe the unimaginable immensity of whose duration in time and extension in space the natural sciences afford us a progressive revelation, is a Mind or Will even remotely analogous to those minds or wills which in all our experience (other, at any rate, than the experience which we call religious) we know only as associated with a particular kind of animal organism. Nor, indeed, do I myself think that, apart from the experience which we call religious, would it be possible in the long run to maintain the suggestion. But believing, as I do, some measure of that experience which we call religious to be a normal feature of human life, I hold that the consciousness of Nature as mediating a Presence, our relation to which is inevitably expressed in language appropriated to intercourse with those who share with us the life of thought and will, is an inalienable and inexpugnable element in our response to our environment. That Natural Science should not find itself able to confirm those facts of religious experience which support the affirmation that we may stand in a personal relation to the object of that experience—and this is, I think, what is meant when theists speak of God as personal —this is not to be wondered at. If I may be allowed to conclude this Lecture by quoting words of my own used elsewhere.[1] Even in the world of objects Science with its generalizing method can only use the *individual* as a point of departure, and the *person*, as the individual subject of knowledge, is doubly unamenable to scientific treatment. A personal relation to the Supreme Reality, such as is expressed in theistic religion, is still further removed from the possibility of such treatment; for here Personality is expressly contem-

[1] *Divine Personality and Human Life*, pp. 72–4. The passage is quoted with some additions and modifications.

plated in union with that ultimate nature of the Whole which is the concern of Philosophy as distinguished from Science by being interested not merely in the world of objects, but in the Whole wherein the known is not severed from the knower, or the object from the subject. There is thus nothing to excite surprise in the appearance of irrelevance to the scientific view of the world which is sometimes—indeed often—felt to attach to the thought of a God with whom personal intercourse is possible. On the other hand, if we start from this thought itself, we may find that this same aversion to it on the part of Science may serve as a means of purifying and enriching the very conception which Science seems to reject.

The late Baron von Hügel profoundly observed that the part played in the religious life of another age by the vision of the Last Judgment has now to a great extent devolved upon the spectacle presented to us by Natural Science of the material universe, extended without bounds in space and enduring from eternity to eternity under the reign of inviolable laws whereby every detail of its course is—or was until the other day—conceived to be determined. If some of the recent speculations of physicists and astronomers have made this description of the scientific view of the world less acceptable than would have been the case a few years ago, yet, even the vision of "the mysterious universe," which the exponents of these new conceptions set before us may well accomplish more thoroughly than the old eschatology the task which it has taken over from it of reducing to insignificance and convicting of vanity the everyday life of human beings. That this task, however, should be performed as efficiently as may be is a matter in which Religion itself is profoundly interested. The feeling which frequently inspires some of the most active hostility encountered by religious tradition among us, the feeling that the conception of God offered to us by that tradition is unworthy of the awful majesty, the immeasurable vastness of this stupendous universe, whose secrets the devotees of Science are ever exploring without any fear of exhausting them—this feeling is in a most true sense a *religious* feeling; and Religion, this feeling once brought home to it, can never be fully content with accepting a God to worship regarding whom a doubt must lurk in the hearts of all but his most ignorant worshippers, whether he is not on a scale, so to speak, quite out of proportion to the world with which the natural sciences acquaint us, and proportioned only to a picture of that world which with the increase of our knowledge we have long since outgrown.

In Science therefore, and in those very characteristics of Science which cause it to take little or no account of Personality, and which often arouse on the part of men imbued with the scientific temper a sharp opposition to Religion itself, and especially to Religion in its theistic form, Religion, and theistic Religion in particular, may come to recognize no irreconcilable enemy, but rather an indispensable helper in the work of enlarging her own conceptions to match the demands of that aspiration after the Highest, and nothing short of the Highest, which is the mainspring of her own activity.

# III

# RELIGION WITHOUT THEISM

## B. HUMANISM

MY third Lecture I propose to devote to the consideration of some attempts to satisfy those deeply rooted demands of human nature which have throughout the history of our race led to the framing of religious systems without depressing the dignity and impairing the independence of that nature by the acknowledgment of its subordination to a Being possessing in a higher degree than itself the attributes of reason and freedom which are its prerogatives among the inhabitants of this planet. Although not peculiar to the present age, such attempts may fairly be said to be characteristic of it. Impatience not of any particular authority, but of authority as such is, I think, unmistakably a feature of the feeling and thought of the generation which regards itself as, in the phrase of the day, "post-war"; although the future historian of ideas will certainly find that this turn of thought was already evident before the outbreak of the World War, however much that great upheaval may have made it more general and determined its subsequent form. This generation does not appeal from human authority to divine or from that of a monarch or aristocracy to that of a People; it does not set up the crown against the mitre, or the mitre against the crown: but rather it claims to have been, like Dante in the Earthly Paradise "crowned and mitred over itself."[1]

I have chosen for special study, as illustrating the tendency I have just been endeavouring to describe, two books which have attracted much attention, although, in my judgment, of very unequal merit and importance. Mr. Walter Lippmann's *Preface to Ethics* is the work of an American author who reflects a mood of the moment without, I venture to think, evincing either an adequate comprehension of the difficulties inherent in the position which he defends, or such knowledge of what has in the past been thought upon the subject of his choice as might have emancipated him from what may perhaps be called without offence a journalistic pride in his modernity. The *Ethics* of Professor Nicolai Hartmann, of Berlin, recently translated into English by Dr. Stanton Coit, is, on the other hand, a highly important contribution to the literature of moral philosophy, combining learning with originality and acute criticism with genuine insight into

[1] *Purg.* xxvii. 142.

moral experience. Both, indeed, are concerned with Ethics rather than with Religion; both, however, suggest a view of the world which may supply to the theory of conduct a background such as Theism has provided in the past, but in their authors' judgment can no longer provide: and such a view is at any rate a substitute for Religion, and may be fairly classed for our purposes as a form of Religion without Theism.

Mr. Lippmann indeed does in one passage[1] claim for his own ideal of human behaviour that it is a religion; he even remarks that "it may be called the religion of the spirit"; and he seems to regard it as consisting in "taking seriously what the world's greatest teachers have said." Of their sayings, the one which apparently commends itself most to himself is one attributed to Confucius, describing it as the goal of human effort " to follow what the heart desires without transgressing what is right;" and this, he would seem to suppose, is equivalent to following whatever an intellectually "mature" human being desires, since he tells us[2] that "a mature desire is innocent." "Maturity" is for Mr. Lippmann a word to conjure with, and it is important for the understanding of his view to be clear as to what he understands by it. Perhaps we find the fullest account of

[1] Page 329. [2] Page 192.

this in words used of a man who is "wholly an adult."[1] "He has conquered mortality in the only way mortal men can conquer it. For he has ceased to expect anything of the world which it cannot give, and he has learned to love it under the only aspect in which it is eternal." It is the "function of high religion," according to our author,[2] "to reveal to men the quality of mature experience," being itself "a prophecy and an anticipation of what life is like when desire is in perfect harmony with reality."

This doctrine of "maturity" as the goal of human life is the first point to which I wish to call attention in Mr. Lippmann's creed. It is not peculiar to him; it, or something like it, is frequently met with in what I may call the literary philosophy (by which I do not mean the philosophical literature) of the day. The apostles of "maturity" sometimes quote as their text the concluding words of Edgar's speech in *King Lear*[3] to his blinded father, when he shows signs of reluctance to prolong his life:

> What, in ill-thoughts again? Men must endure
> Their going hence even as their coming hither,
> *Ripeness is all*,

and invite us to see in them a declaration of Shakespeare's own final attitude towards human life. I am

[1] Page 191. [2] Page 193. [3] Act. v. sc. 2.

not at all sure that this is not to lay a greater stress upon them than they were ever meant by their author to bear; but this is, no doubt, often the case with sermon-texts. We have already seen how Mr. Lippmann would define "maturity." His definition had two parts. The former, "not to expect anything of the world which it cannot give," seems to mean much what is expressed in the phrase often used of an experienced man of the world—"He has no illusions"; the latter, "to have learned to love the world in the only aspect in which it is eternal," sounds like an echo of Spinoza's *amor intellectualis Dei*, to which I have already referred in my previous Lecture, while the definition as a whole reminds one of the same philosopher's warning, also mentioned before, that a man, in loving God, must not look for God to love him in return.

The word "maturity," however, has a biological reference which is, I think, alien from Spinoza's conception of the eternity which man inherits, when he is emancipated from his passions, and finds his satisfaction in a life of understanding crowned by disinterested love of that which is understood. For this is possible to us because we are not only members of an animal species, with a natural course of development which every individual of the species, if not prematurely cut off, must traverse in its turn, but also intelligences which are, in Spinoza's own phrase, "part of the infinite understanding of God." Moreover, it is legitimate to suspect, even in Spinoza himself, great thinker as he unquestionably is, a discordance between his general theory and the religious enthusiasm in which his contemplation of Reality culminates; and to wonder whether the latter does not in fact draw its inspiration less from his own philosophy than from the spiritual experience of his people, that people which has been, in the words of Athanasius, the school of the knowledge of God to all nations; an experience which was essentially an experience not of an eternal Order, but of a living God, the "lover of souls." Certainly Mr. Lippmann ignores this experience; and, while he is doubtless justified in thinking that acquiescence in certain traditional representations of that which is this experienced is, for sundry reasons, more difficult for men and women of to-day than it was for their ancestors, he tends to forget that "faith" is not, as he is apt to imply, a name for such acquiescence, but for a spiritual activity which, as those who have known it best have ever been aware, is in its own nature difficult, and that just because of the defiance of what is "seen"—of the obvious appearances of the world about it—which it has involved, not only since the

World War, but from the days of the author of the Book of Job, and doubtless from a far more remote antiquity than his.

More interesting and original, however, in my judgment, than Mr. Lippmann's stress on "maturity" —a word the familiarity of which in its purely biological sense hides from the reader the absence of any adequate discussion by the author of its precise significance when used of mind or spirit—is his suggestion that the mentality of the present generation is alienated from Theism by what he calls "machine technology." Of this he tells us[1] that, "as it makes social relations complex, it dissolves the habits of obedience and dependence; it dissipates the centralization of power and of leadership; it diffuses the experience of responsible decision throughout the population, compelling each man to acquire the habit of making judgments instead of looking for orders, of adjusting his will to the will of others instead of trusting to custom and organized loyalties. The real law," Mr. Lippmann continues, "under which modern society is administered is neither the accumulated precedents of tradition nor a set of commands originating on high which are imposed like orders on the rank and file below. The real law in the modern State is the multitude of

[1] Pages 274–5.

decisions made by millions of men." By the side of this passage I will quote another[1]: "If the modern man is an optimist on the subject of his impulses" (and therefore, to supply the context of this remark, unwilling readily to accept an ethical tradition which seems to treat those impulses with suspicion) "the reason is to be found less in his own self-confidence than in his distrust of men and in his intoxication over things."

Now we may not unreasonably ask whether "humanism" can be the right name for the view of life expressed in this last paragraph, and which, it cannot, I think, be denied, is very prevalent in those urbanized communities which (as Mr. Lippmann has observed) are specially typical of contemporary civilization. ("Our own civilization in America," he says, "is the most completely urbanized of all.") Would not this view of life be more properly described by some term suggesting that neither God nor man, but, as a countryman of Mr. Lippmann's has said, "*things* are in the saddle, and ride mankind"?

There is no doubt little in the environment of peoples whose main concern is with machines to keep them in touch either with ancient religious institutions historically associated with occupations organized in an age preceding that in which those machines were

[1] Page 158.

invented, or with what Mr. Lippmann speaks of[1] as "the deep and abiding traditions of religion" which "belong to the countryside," where "a man earns his daily bread by submitting to superhuman forces whose behaviour he can only partially control" (I should rather say "can only control to a very small degree," for surely even over his own machines his control is limited by the laws of their material.)

That the thought of God, therefore, should be strange and unfamiliar to men thus cut off from the surroundings which have in the past most powerfully suggested it to others is nothing wonderful. But only a somewhat naïve confidence, such as Mr. Lippmann's, in the finality or, as he would say, "maturity" of the mentality of his own generation, can justify an assurance that humanity at large will or can ultimately dispense with an idea which in some form or other has been so intimately bound up with its development. It is probable enough that the religion of the future will in some way, at which, being no prophet, I make no pretence of guessing, bear traces of the age of machines as the religion of the present does of the ages which preceded it; and will therein be different from the religion of those ages and of this age. But it is likely to be precisely the issue of the domination of

[1] Page 62.

machines in modern life that "humanism" will be found inadequate to the needs of a generation which, having, according to Mr. Lippmann himself, learned to distrust men "in its intoxication over things," may reawaken to the possibilities of direct contact with a Spiritual Reality through communion wherewith man may be emancipated from the slavery that threatens us to-day to things which are less than human and are, indeed, like the idols of old, the work of men's hands.

I do not think, from some observations of Mr. Lippmann himself, that he would expect such emancipation from a "religion of humanity" like that of Comte, with a reference to which these lectures began, or like that which will be found eloquently described in the writings of W. K. Clifford, to which I referred in my second Lecture; a religion which, while rejecting faith in a God beyond humanity, would deify our own race conceived as an ideal unity, manifested indeed in a succession of passing individuals, but enduring although they pass. Such a religion of humanity, indeed, Mr. Lippmann thinks, "is wholly unacceptable to those who have to ride in the subways during the rush hour." But some who agree with him in regarding Theism as a creed outworn, think more nobly of humanity than Mr. Lippmann; and to one of these, Professor Nicolai Hartmann, of Berlin, I now turn. His rejection of Theism, at any rate as a doctrine of any significance for the understanding of the principles of human conduct, is actually determined by his profound sense of the dignity of human nature as invested with the freedom and autonomy presupposed by man's moral consciousness; a dignity which appears to Professor Hartmann to be incompatible with that sense of dependence on God in which, we may remind ourselves, the most influential theologian of his country in modern times—Schleiermacher—placed the essence of religion.

Were my subject Ethics, I should be disposed to linger over Professor Hartmann's book, which seems to me, as I have already said, the most important contribution to that subject that has for some time past come under my notice; but I am only here concerned with the attitude of the author towards Theism; between which and any philosophy which will square with the moral consciousness of man he believes an irreconcilable contradiction to exist. This attitude of Professor Hartmann may seem all the more remarkable because his own conception of the moral consciousness is admittedly very close to that of Kant, who, as is well known, while unable to regard as cogent the traditional arguments for the existence of God from the constitution of the world and of the human mind, held that an adequate ground of belief therein was to be discovered in the demands of this same moral consciousness. It will, however, be present to the recollection of those who are familiar with Kant's ethical teaching and with the criticisms on it which are current in treatises on moral philosophy, that it is no new thing to hold that he was betrayed (perhaps, as the poet Heine humorously suggested, by consideration for the pious feelings of his old servant Lampe) into a fatal inconsistency with his own insistence on the absolute disinterestedness necessary to any morally good action or relation, when he introduced into his system, as a postulate (to use his own expression) of the practical reason (as he called the moral consciousness), the thought of a Being possessed of the will and power to crown with happiness hereafter the virtue which is so often in this life left unrewarded.

But this is not the line taken by Professor Hartmann. On the contrary, he does greater justice to Kant's argument on this subject than has often been done to it by its critics. For he fully recognizes that, as he puts it,[1] it is of the essence of moral goodness to be worthy of happiness, that is to say, that whatever of paradox we may find in the circumstance, the claim

[1] English tr., Vol. II, p. 148.

of virtue to happiness is no less bound up with our consciousness of moral obligation than is the disclaimer of happiness as the determining motion of any act which can properly be called virtuous. Professor Hartmann does not, then, differ from Kant, in admitting that not only do virtuous people, like others, *wish* to be happy, but the conscience of men in general, whether virtuous or no, informs them that virtue deserves happiness; where he differs from Kant is in the fact that he is content to say that this merited happiness of the virtuous is a *desideratum* and to leave it there; while Kant sees in this deliverance of conscience, which both he and Professor Hartmann recognize, a prophecy of the fulfilment of its demand, and therefore an evidence of the existence of one who can fulfil it.

But Professor Hartmann goes further than a refusal to follow Kant in a line of argument which at first sight strikes one as artificial and precarious, and which perhaps few readers of Kant have found satisfactory. He does not indeed seem impressed as much as some other contemporary critics of Theism by the incongruity between the view of the world suggested by the present conclusions of science, natural and historical, and the idea of a transcendent Governor of the universe of whom we may speak in personal terms.

Rather does he, in the fashion of an earlier agnosticism, indeed of Kant himself, talk of God's existence and even of his providence as of what can neither be proved nor disproved.[1] Yet, unlike Kant, he has certainly (as people say nowadays) "no use for" an hypothesis which he considers in any case unverifiable. For, as we have already seen, he regards it as essentially inconsistent with the data of that very moral consciousness, as a "postulate" of which Kant was prepared to defend it. But not only does Professor Hartmann agree with Kant in the premises of the latter's argument for the existence of God, though refusing to draw Kant's, or indeed any conclusion from them, he constantly uses language which seems to cry out for a belief in God to give it meaning. Thus we read[2] that moral passion "springs from reverence for the unbounded abundance of the things that are of worth; it is knowledge filled with gratitude, and, where knowledge fails, it is the presentiment that the values of existence are inexhaustible"; and, again, that "pure joy in everything which is worthy of joy culminates ultimately in a deep sentiment of gratitude, in a great and profound sense of reverential wonder at the richness of life."[3] But to whom is this

[1] Vol. I, p. 270; Vol. III, p. 282. [2] Vol. I, p. 210.
[3] Ibid., p. 243.

gratitude, this reverence, of which Professor Hartmann speaks, to be felt? for these are surely sentiments which demand a personal object. And if the obvious reply is "to God," so, too, a presentiment of the inexhaustibleness of the values of existence can with difficulty be distinguished from faith in the goodness of God, and can find a rational justification only in the consciousness of communion with such a Being as we commonly mean when we speak of God—an infinite Goodness inspiring us with a confidence to which the best analogy is to be sought in the trust created in us by intercourse with a just and sympathetic personality.

The natural sequel of such language as I have quoted from Professor Hartmann is certainly not the repudiation of Theism which we actually find in his book. Rather does the existence of such feelings as *gratitude* and *reverence*, which he so emphatically allows it to be inevitable and right for us to feel—and it is to be noted that he explicitly holds[1] that there is an "a priorism of emotional acts" which "is just as pure, original, autonomous, and transcendental an authority as the logical and categorical a priorism in the domain of theory"—suggest an argument for God's existence such as is outlined in a very remarkable paper on the subject by my own teacher, the late Professor Cook

[1] Vol. I, p. 178.

Wilson, which was posthumously published along with his work on *Statement and Inference*[1]—or as may be found more diffusely elaborated in the two philosophical treatises of James Martineau's old age, *Types of Ethical Theory* and *A Study of Religion.*

I suppose that the answer which Professor Hartmann himself would give to an enquiry after the proper object of the reverence and gratitude which he holds to be features of the morally right attitude would be that it is the "eternal values," which in his system remind us of—and indeed are expressly identified with—the Forms or Ideas of the Platonic philosophy. Lofty as is his conception of human dignity, he tells us that "man does not feel humility in the presence of man," but only, it would seem, of the ethical Ideal.

But I cannot rid myself of the conviction that the attitude thus considered appropriate to these Ideas or Values does after all involve precisely such a "personification" of them in relation to ourselves as is in fact equivalent to the affirmation of personality in God, when this is taken, as I have elsewhere[2] contended at length that it should be taken, not as an arbitrary transference to the infinite and absolute Reality of

[1] Vol. II, pp. 835 ff.

[2] In my Gifford Lectures on *God and Personality* and *Divine Personality and Human Life*.

predicates essentially finite and relative, but as the inevitable expression of an actual religious experience of that Reality by individual persons.

Not only, however, does Professor Hartmann use language which is left by his rejection of Theism hanging, as it were, in the air, we find him afterwards criticizing the ethical teaching of Christianity on what appear to be two mutually contradictory grounds; and here again we shall find, I think, the source of the confusion (as I take it to be) in a misapprehension by the author of the true nature of the Theism which, as found in Christianity, he holds to be inadmissible from the point of view of a genuinely ethical view of human life.

He recognizes the service rendered by Christianity to ethics in its assertion of the value of "brotherly love"—by which is plainly meant the *ἀγάπη* of the second great commandment of the New Testament, the practical—not emotional—love of one's neighbour as oneself—in its distinction from "personal love," that is, presumably the *ἔρως* of the ancients, which cannot be "commanded" at all.[1] I will not stop here to dwell upon the consideration that "commanded," a word freely used by Professor Hartmann, is at least more suggestive of a "theistic" than of a

[1] Vol. III, p. 456.

"humanistic" background to the ethical teaching in which it occurs. The point to which I wish now to call attention is that Professor Hartmann qualifies his acknowledgement of the contribution of Christianity to moral philosophy in this matter of "brotherly love" by the remark that "one cannot maintain that this value was brought in its full purity, that is, in its complete autonomy, into current acceptance by Christianity. In it there stood behind brotherly love the love of God, which no longer has the ethical impress. In his neighbour the Christian loves the Christian God."[1]

The truth of this last observation I am not concerned to deny. But I would have you note our author's dogmatic assertion that the love of God "has no longer the ethical impress." What Professor Hartmann intends to convey by this remark is that, for him, as we shall shortly see, ethics or morality is essentially a matter of relations between human beings. The love of God he does not, if I understand him, conceive to be possibly a sentiment characterized by that disinterestedness which he follows Kant in holding to be the hall-mark of whatever has a genuinely moral value. The position of the "love of God" in Christian ethics therefore, in his view, inevitably imports into it a non-moral element. "The altruism," he says,[2] "of this

[1] Vol. II, p. 278.

[2] Vol. I, p. 135.

world is at the same time egoism as regards the Beyond. Here is the point in which the Christian must necessarily be an egoist and an eudaemonist, on the basis of his religious metaphysic of the Beyond. This is no external accompaniment of Christian ethics. It inheres in the essence of the matter. Man is answerable before God for his own action, but only for his own. The conduct of his fellow-man is withdrawn from his volition. Accordingly he can care only for his own salvation."

It is not, after reading such passages as the last two quoted, altogether without surprise that we find Professor Hartmann criticizing this same Christian morality which has, according to him, allowed its "metaphysic of the Beyond," as he calls it, to spoil its ethics of "brotherly love," on the ground that[1] "the mistake of Christianity is the belief that the moral law depends upon brotherly love alone." He here seems altogether to overlook (and the oversight is not peculiar to him) what he has nevertheless previously, in another connexion, noted as a flaw in Christian ethics; namely, the "first great commandment" of love to God, which in Jesus' summary of the law is placed beside and before that "like unto it" of brotherly love for our neighbour. For surely what he himself goes on to

[1] Vol. II, p. 463.

describe under the name of "the love of the remotest" is no other than the very thing which that "first commandment" requires. Professor Hartmann describes it[1] as involving a "great venture" to which "only a deep and mighty faith is equal," "faith of a unique kind, different from trust between man and man; a faith which reaches out to the whole of things, and can do no other than stake what it has." What is this but precisely that love of God with all our heart and soul and mind and strength, in which Christianity finds the complement, or rather the basis, of the brotherly love, wherein lies the essence of our duty to our neighbour?

Professor Hartmann would no doubt refuse to identify his "love of the remotest" with the Christian "love of God" because he is, I venture to think, obsessed by the thought that the God of religion must be "too much a man"[2] not to be a competitor with man for the love which we owe our fellows. Yet his own "Remotest," if it is to be the object of "love," must surely be envisaged so far "anthropomorphically" as to admit of the direction toward it of a sentiment primarily, at any rate, personal in its reference. To me

[1] Vol. II, p. 330.

[2] I am thinking of Matthew Arnold's praise of Goethe, who "neither made man too much a God, Or God too much a man."

it seems that this insistence on the necessity of finding a place in our morality for the "love of the remotest" is in fact a recognition at least that morality cannot but in the long run involve Religion, and, if we are to do full justice to the implications of the thought, not Religion only but Theism. The first great commandment of the Christian law means for me, as I have elsewhere put it, "that morality rests upon a principle transcending the individual consciousness and belonging to the spiritual principle of unity in all reality, a principle conceived of in Christianity as revealing its nature in the experience of mutual love." This truth, as I take it to be, "cannot be disregarded without imperilling morality" itself. "In other words, morality cannot dispense with Religion; not in the sense that it requires an external sanction, but in the sense that, except as interpreted by Religion, it must appear as an unintelligible fact, incoherent with the rest of experience, and so come easily to be suspected of being no more than an obstinate prejudice which the wise man will endeavour to disregard."[1]

The expression of this truth in the first of the two great commandments which summarize Christian morality by the requirement to love not an abstraction but a personal Being seems to me not an instance of

[1] *Contribution of Christianity to Ethics*, p. 116.

what Professor Hartmann somewhere calls contemptuously "anthropocentric megalomania," but a reasonable acquiescence in the powerful suggestions made by the sentiments of "gratitude," "reverence," and "love," which, as Professor Hartmann fully recognizes, arise spontaneously in our hearts under circumstances which cannot, after all, be more adequately described than in the traditional language which speaks of a divine Presence revealed in nature or in conscience—that is, to quote once more Kant's famous phrase, by the "starry heavens above," or "the moral law within."

What is it, then, that induces Professor Hartmann to refuse such acquiescence, and that in the name of morality? It is, as we have already seen, his profound conviction that to allow to the idea of God any place in ethics is an outrage on the majority of human nature. "That anything whatsoever in heaven or on the earth, even though it be God himself, should take precedence of Man, would be ethically perverse; it would not be moral; it would be treason to mankind, which must rely upon itself alone."[1]

Although myself on the contrary no less profoundly convinced of the opposite, it would be idle to deny that Theism may be and has been presented in forms, in which it really does make it difficult to find room for

[1] Vol. III, p. 264.

God in one and the same intelligible world with man, if man is to be allowed to possess that autonomy and freedom which is, as Kant and Professor Hartmann in accordance with common sense agree, a "postulate" of morality; that is, must belong to man, if moral responsibility is to be reckoned other than an illusion.

In what remains of this third Lecture, I will endeavour to put as fairly as I can the main points made by Professor Hartmann against the compatibility of Theism with an ethical theory which shall do justice to man's moral freedom and responsibility; reserving any reply which I have to make to my final Lecture which, according to my programme, is to be devoted to a vindication of Theism.

Professor Hartmann is not greatly concerned with what is probably the most obvious objection that can be raised against Theism from an ethical point of view; namely, that if an action be supposed to be right because commanded by God, we might be morally obliged to do or approve something repugnant to our moral sense because God had chosen to command it. It was in view of this objection that Kant shows himself so anxious to make it clear that, although we may conveniently regard moral laws as divine commands, we must recognize that we know them to be commands of God because our conscience perceives them to be morally obligatory, and not the other way round. But, in consequence of the influence of the Kantian ethics, few philosophical theists would now be disposed to find the standard of morality in the arbitrary will of God; and at any rate it is not against a view of this kind that Professor Hartmann chiefly directs his polemic. Yet when he affirms[1] that Religion necessarily denies the independence of morality; that "according to its way of thinking all morality is only a means," he must have in view a not wholly dissimilar position. A passage already quoted, in which "the altruism of this world" is said to be "at the same time egoism as regards the Beyond" seems to suggest that he is thinking of God, not indeed as an arbitrary despot who may capriciously give mutually contradictory orders, but at any rate as One with whom each religious individual seeks communion for himself, regarding his fellows as merely instrumental in fitting him for such communion. The edge of this criticism may be turned by a less purely transcendent conception of God than that which Professor Hartmann seems habitually to contemplate; a conception of him as, on the one hand, revealing his own nature in the moral law recognized by our conscience, and as, on the other, immanent in

[1] Vol. I, p. 110.

the human brethren who are the immediate objects of our moral activity.

The point on which Professor Hartmann lays most stress is not the inconsistency between the notion of a divine legislator anthropomorphically imagined and that of a moral law intuitively apprehended by the reason and conscience of man, but the impossibility of accommodating human morality to a world teleologically ordered to ends recognized by the human mind as right to propose to oneself, and therefore presumably so ordered by a Mind appreciative of the same values as the human. I will content myself here with setting out this contention of Professor Hartmann's, and examine, so far as I can, its cogency in my concluding Lecture, which will be occupied by a defence of the general position impugned by Professor Hartmann, as well as by the authors previously discussed.

"The whole significance of morality is abolished" (says Professor Hartmann[1]) "if freedom be proved to be an illusion." But, he thinks, freedom could be no other than an illusion if "the teleology of the existential process were ontologically fixed"; or, in less technical language, if what *ought* to be *must* by a natural necessity be, as, supposing the world to be determined "teleologically" or "finalistically" by a "moral Governor"

[1] Vol. III, p. 23.

such as God is conceived to be, must inevitably be the case. On the other hand, if the world be *causally* determined throughout, the results of our voluntary activity will be what *must* be if we so will and act, but may or not be what *ought* to be according as we will and act rightly or wrongly. Professor Hartmann does not indeed, any more than his predecessors in the field of ethical speculation, succeed in eliminating all mystery from the situation created by the presence in a world throughout causally determined of the freedom to determine our action this way or that which moral responsibility seems to involve. Yet he holds not only that, as he truly says, "a free will with its finalistic mode of efficacy is possible only in a world entirely determined causally," since otherwise one could not depend upon one's actions bringing about the intended result; but that a "finalistic" or "teleological" activity can be "inserted" (the expression is his own) into a causally determined world, otherwise indifferent to morality and so capable of being what he calls "axiologically" though not ontologically determined (determined as regards *value*, that is, not as regards *fact*) by the mind of man in particular cases, as it could not be inserted in one wherein the sequence of events was *already* axiologically determined to the ends we should regard as the best. When such a determination of the sequence of events has been asserted, as by some idealistic thinkers, whether the determining power has been conceived as a personal God or otherwise, morality has, he thinks, always tended to pass into a so-called "higher morality," not of free choice, but of acquiescence in the actual, which is considered to be what God wills, or what ought to be. Such a "higher morality" is, Professor Hartmann holds, no morality at all, lacking as it does the essential character of freedom to choose what from a moral point ought not to be. This is an argument, as I have already hinted, and as our author himself points out, not merely against Theism, but against any view of the world as a "realm of ends," to use a Kantian phrase, which has been adopted by James Ward among recent English philosophers to express his own conception of the ultimate nature of reality. It is often suggested that it is precisely in a world conceived as such a "realm of ends" that human morality would be, so to say, at home, while in a mechanically determined system of causes and effects it must be a stranger and an alien. Professor Hartmann's contention is diametrically the reverse of this. Not a mechanically determined system of events, including within itself some with a special character imparted to them by our valuation of them as right or wrong, good or bad, but one in which "whatever is, is right," because ordered to good ends by a God or some Principle tantamount to a God, is in our author's view the kind of world which leaves no room for morality. For morality implies a human nature free to choose between good and evil in an order of things where every cause is infallibly followed by its effect, whether that effect be good or whether it be evil: and how can any effect be really evil where nothing can happen but in accordance with the providence of God?

## IV

# PSYCHOLOGICAL ACCOUNTS OF THE ORIGIN OF BELIEF IN GOD

THE authors whom I have selected for discussion in the foregoing pages have, as we have seen, assailed Theism as, on the one hand, exalting our human nature overmuch by envisaging the ultimate power in the universe in the likeness of man and, on the other hand, degrading this same human nature of ours by refusing to recognize it as, in its kind, the most exalted thing within our experience, with nothing above it to which that kind of respect which we are accustomed to pay to it might be due in a higher degree. These arguments of theirs against belief in God, mutually opposed, though perhaps not mutually contradictory, do not appear to depend upon any particular theory of the origin of that belief. But I do not think it can be reasonably denied that the wide acceptance with which such a rejection of Theism as they champion undoubtedly meets among our educated contemporaries is greatly promoted by the general prevalence of an impression that psychologists, exploring (whether by the method specifically known as psycho-analysis or otherwise) the constitution of the human mind, have found an adequate explanation of the origin of the belief in a God or gods and of the *consensus gentium* to which that belief can unquestionably appeal, as an illusion almost inevitably generated at a certain stage of culture by the circumstances affecting that mind's development. The present chapter will be devoted to a brief consideration of this alleged explanation and of its sufficiency to invalidate the conviction of which it professes to exhibit the genesis.

No attempt will be made here, nor am I competent to make such an attempt, to examine the credentials of psycho-analysis as a method of therapeutics, or as a means of ascertaining the antecedents in the lives of individuals which are causally connected with their sentiments, habits, and beliefs. It is obvious that, apart from confirmation which can rarely be had, the evidence afforded by a psychotherapist's interpretation of another person's dreams, or of what may be elicited from his patients, whether under hypnosis or by the method of "free association," as to events in forgotten periods of their infancy may be exposed to much justifiable scepticism. But, so far as I can venture to express an opinion, the light which has been shown by the investigations of psycho-analysis upon the genesis of phenomena in the lives of us all to which but little attention had previously been paid, is too great to permit of a wholesale rejection of theories which yet, as advanced by their best-known exponents, are fertile in mythology, and stand in much need of a strict philosophical criticism.

The discussion of them in this chapter will, however, make no pretence of supplying this latter criticism. I shall confine myself to indicating what seem to me to be limits set by the nature of things to the availability of such methods as psycho-analysts pursue for the interpretation of human thought; and in so doing, to suggesting that such interpretation is not to be had from psychology alone, of whatever school. In this connexion it will be necessary to say something of theories which, although not based upon the special doctrines of the psycho-analytic school, agree with those so based in finding, if not in religion in general, at any rate in the belief in God, an illusion susceptible of being dispelled by a more thorough acquaintance with the laws governing the genesis and development of the human mind, individual and social. Such a theory is, for example, maintained with much ability, on a basis of wide reading in the records of religious experience, by Professor Leuba, who is by no means prepared to adhere to the particular views characteristic of any school of psycho-analysts.

It has been explained in the first Lecture that the special subject of this book is the rejection of Theism by thinkers who are not concerned to reject Religion in every sense of the word. In taking this as our theme, we have already found some difficulty in ascertaining its limits. This difficulty has arisen from the fact that many, both among the opponents and among the defenders of religion, are in the habit of associating it so closely with a belief in a God or gods that they cannot recognize as entitled to bear the name any view which is expressly atheistical. Nor is anyone who (like the present writer) holds that belief in God is characteristic of the highest form taken by religion concerned to deny that there is much justification for this habit. Yet the history of religion makes it impossible to deny that an attitude towards life which is essentially religious may be found apart from any explicit belief in the existence of a being or beings to whom the name would naturally be applied; and this book is primarily concerned with a mode of thought which allows such an attitude apart from such a belief to be reasonable. We are now, it is true, about to discuss certain views of the origin of the belief in God which imply, I think, that religion, in any sense which claims to place us in relation with a sphere of being inacessible to exploration by the methods appropriate to the natural sciences, is of necessity an illusion. But the most eminent upholders of these views are ready to admit that the part played by religion in the past as a guide to human life has been largely beneficial, and that it is a matter of urgency that, in a world where (as they hold) the belief in a God or gods which has so often, if not always, been bound up with religion is destined to disappear before the advance of science, a motive power should be discovered which, apart from any such belief, may accomplish—perhaps better than religion has ever actually succeeded in accomplishing—the function, so far performed, when performed at all, by religion, of establishing, amid the changes and chances of human life and the fears and distractions which these inspire, a much-needed sense of confidence and unity in the life alike of societies and of individuals.

How then, we may begin our task by enquiring, is religion held to have hitherto performed, or essayed to perform, this important function? In the main, by setting before men the image of a Being who, wearing their own likeness, and capable, like another human being, of arousing the emotions of fear and love, is both—to use a phrase often employed by Professor Pratt in his valuable work on *The Religious Consciousness*—"the determiner of destiny" and the controller of their environment. The belief in such a being becomes, no doubt, increasingly difficult as it becomes more and more plain that there is no such empirical evidence of his existence as there is in the case of other objects of our fear and love, whose bodies we can see with our eyes, whose voices we can hear with our ears, and with whom we can enjoy mutual converse. "No man"—the saying is not, we may note, that of an atheist, but of a New Testament writer[1]—"hath seen God at any time." The imaginations of God are traced either to a "sense of presence" due to peculiar conditions of the worshipper's own mind and feelings, or (as with Freud) to memories of our parents as they appeared to us in our infancy. With the discovery of the illusory nature of any belief in the reality of the Being thus imagined, the power of such a belief to discharge the useful functions in the economy of human life which it discharged in the past must decay and perish, to be replaced, if at all, by a comprehension of the attainable aims which a man can set before himself, and an agreement with our fellows to order our lives so as to promote those which may afford us such satisfaction in the present and assurance of satisfaction in the future as the conditions of our existence permit.

[1] John i. 18.

Within the limits at my disposal it is impossible to do more than offer some observations upon these psychological explanations of the origin of the idea of God which, whatever their differences in detail, agree in denying objective validity to this idea. These observations will be directed to suggesting, not that the facts brought to our notice by psychologists do not contribute much that is of value for our better understanding of our religious experience, but that they do not really dispose of its claims to be a genuine experience of a reality other than our own "psyche" or soul. I shall endeavour to show that the assumption of such a reality in the case of God is parallel assumptions made by the critics of Theism themselves in other cases. I shall point out that the explanations offered by psychologists of the nature of the idea of God do not answer the question about the origin of that idea put by such thinkers as Descartes, who found no satisfactory solution except in the assertion of the reality of such a Being as the idea in question represents to us. I shall suggest that certain facts about the mystic's "sense of presence" which appear to Professor Leuba to rule it out as evidence of the reality of a "transcendental object" are not incompatible with taking that "sense" along with other features of our religious consciousness as contributory testimony to the reality of our communion with a God who is no mere fantasy of our own creating. Lastly, I shall attempt to argue that the connexion which is not to be denied (and which indeed is openly emphasized in many authoritative expressions of religious experience) between the child's attitude to his parents and the mature man or woman's attitude to God is susceptible of an explanation which in no way necessitates the atheistical conclusion which has been drawn from the psychological premises.

To the remarks, the general character of which I have now outlined, I will prefix a short consideration of what appears to me to be a caution very requisite to be borne in mind in dealing with all psychology, whether it be that which (until some other school shall arise with a better claim to the designation —for we can scarcely expect that it will, like Newcastle-on-Tyne, or New College at Oxford, retain it when invested with the glamour of a venerable antiquity) rejoices in the title of the "new pyschology," or whether it be that of a period as yet ignorant of the methods of psycho-analysis. I mean that, while it is obvious that, of all the activities of the human soul (if, waiving certain familiar objections, we may provisionally so call that with which the science of psychology is concerned), none is more important than *knowledge*;

nevertheless, any psychology which, following the precedent of the other "natural" sciences, ignores questions which are strictly rather philosophical than "scientific," must inevitably be embarrassed by the appearance of this activity among the phenomena with which it has to deal. For, from the nature of the case, it can only trace out the antecedents of knowledge in individual cases, and describe what (so to put it) it feels like to know. Yet knowledge must have a reference external to itself; one cannot know what is not real, and as it will scarcely be denied that men sometimes suppose themselves to know when they do not, a criterion would seem to be imperatively demanded by which genuine knowledge may be discriminated from pretenders to the name. The psychologist may indeed be at first inclined to say that this discrimination is not his business; that, as a psychologist, he is no more concerned with the problem of the nature of knowledge as such than is the chemist or the mathematician. Yet he cannot, we may say with confidence, maintain this position to the end. The chemist or the mathematician assumes throughout that his investigations, rightly pursued, lead to knowledge; but knowledge is not a function or activity of the very object which he is investigating, while, in the case of the psychologist, it is certainly such. At the same time he must, like every other man of science, assume that there is such a thing as knowledge; for, except upon this assumption, his own investigations have no *raison d'être*; and hence it is not open to him to regard it as an open question whether the phenomena of knowing, or those of believing, doubting, and so forth, which derive their whole significance from their relation to knowledge, have any objective reference. For his own proceedings, and those of every scientific enquirer, would be mere "sound and fury, signifying nothing," unless the possibility of knowledge and our acquaintance with its nature be taken for granted at every step. From these considerations it seems to follow that psychology cannot dispense with the recognition, in the soul which is the object of its study, of something having that *absolute* character which takes us at once out of the sphere of what in modern usage is called "science" into that of philosophy. From reluctance frankly to admit this disturbing peculiarity of their branch of study, and to draw from it would seem to be its inevitable consequence, namely, that psychology can never be a purely "natural science," psychologists are not unnaturally attracted by the thought that "knowledge," so far as they are concerned with it at all, may be identified with correspondence between our thoughts and feelings on one side and sensible experience on the other. It is the seeming refuge offered by this identification from the plunge into the gulf of metaphysical speculation to which their inability to escape the problem of the nature of knowledge invites them that leads to what may well strike us as a strange result. I mean the result that psychologists, such as those of the psycho-analytic school, whose own methods of enquiry would seem to depend entirely upon the recognition of a psychical principle of unity distinct (though not, it may be, separable) from that of the material body, as that is considered apart from the soul which constitutes it not merely a "body" but an "organism," are sometimes found to profess a strict materialism, and to treat perception by the senses as the ultimate test of reality, regardless alike of the liability of the senses themselves to illusion (of which no one can be better aware than such psychologists), and of the difficulty of reconciling with such an outlook any such confidence as they are probably, as a rule, quite ready to place in the conclusions of mathematical science.

I have prefixed these observations to my discussion of the attempts of psychologists to explain the origin of the idea of God because I believe that what I suspect to be a confusion of thought that has haunted psychology throughout the modern period of its history has no small part in disposing psychologists to regard the results of their study of the development of that idea alike in individual minds, and in the traditions of the race as incompatible with belief in an objective reality revealed to us through its presence therein.

We ought, then, to be on our guard against this besetting temptation of psychology, and to recognize that the power of apprehending objective reality, or, in other words, the capacity for knowledge, is an attribute of the human mind which can only be denied to it if we are content to embrace a complete scepticism and empty of all meaning every "science," including the very psychology which has induced our doubts. This recognition by no means carries with it the justification of every claim put forth on behalf of any conviction whatsoever to be an apprehension of objective reality. However great the difficulty which it may present to philosophers, it is impossible to deny the fact of illusion; and the contention that the belief in God rests upon illusion must be dealt with on its own merits.

The best-known exponent of psycho-analysis after Dr. Freud, the celebrated founder of that method, is certainly Dr. Jung. This writer tells us[1] that "every man has eyes and all his senses to perceive that the

[1] *Psychology of the Unconscious*, Eng. tr., p. 30.

world is dead, cold, and unending, and he has never yet seen a God, nor brought to light the existence of such from empirical necessity." We will not now enquire how we perceive with the senses that the world is unending, but we will note that the last clause of the sentence seems to be intended to cover inferences from what is perceptible to the senses to what is not, of the kind which we make when we conclude that the moon has another side than that which we see, though it is never turned towards the earth, and thus is always invisible to human eyes. The purport of the statement is plainly that the senses are the sole source of our knowledge; and that therefore, apart from the testimony of the senses to its existence, or its implication in the existence of what enjoys that testimony, there can be no good reason for believing in the reality of anything which may be alleged to exist. The matter is not, however, so simple as Dr. Jung appears to assume; and I may again remind my readers that, at least according to the teaching of the two religions most widely professed in Europe and America, that is to say, of Christianity and Judaism, it is not only admitted but deliberately proclaimed that God is not an object of the senses. Even when it is held (as in the Aristotelian natural theology at present canonized in the Roman Catholic Church) that all legitimate arguments for his existence have their point of departure in a sensible experience, he is not conceived to be (like the other side of the moon) a possible though not an actual object of sensible experience, such as I take to be in Dr. Jung's mind when he speaks of things "the existence of which is brought to light from empirical necessity."

There are, I suppose, two kinds of being whose existence is almost universally admitted, bodies and minds. I do not speak of laws of thought, mathematical relations, moral principles, or other such objects of thought, the reality of which most of us implicitly, if not explicitly, take for granted; because we do not commonly attribute to these *existence* in the sense in which we suppose ourselves, other people, and the external world to exist. Of the existence, however, of the beings just enumerated the vast majority of mankind entertain no doubt; and these fall into the two classes previously mentioned—bodies and minds. In saying this, no question is begged as to the nature of relations between "bodies" and "minds." It is open to anyone to contend, on the one hand, that what in ourselves and other people we call our minds are no more than effects of the organization of our bodies, or, on the other hand, that bodies exist only when and as apprehended by minds. For even those who take up these positions, which would by most people be regarded as highly paradoxical, must distinguish those qualities of extension, motion, and the like which we attribute to bodies, from those of thinking, feeling, and the like, of which we are aware in ourselves, and which we impute to those whom we take to be our fellows. We can therefore distinguish between the things which exhibit the first set of qualities and those which exhibit the second; although the latter class may eventually turn out to be a part of the former, or the members of the former class to be dependent for their existence upon the members of the latter.

Now it will further be generally admitted that what we call perception by the senses is concerned in our apprehension of both bodies and minds. Bodies are what we see and touch; and though we should not speak of seeing or touching minds, our consciousness of other people's presence is unquestionably mediated to us through our seeing or touching or otherwise sensibly perceiving their bodily forms and movements; while it is not possible to deny that our knowledge of our own selves is in fact intimately bound up both with the experience of seeing and touching our bodies, and still more intimately with the "organic sensations" which we regularly appropriate to ourselves. The assertion that we are ever aware of minds altogether apart from sense perception would be, to say the least, impossible to substantiate; for neither in what is called "telepathy" nor in what is taken by "mystics" for direct communion with God is the activity of sense organs entirely absent.

This being so, it is easy to see how natural it is that people should, like the psychologists whose manner of accounting for the belief in God I am now considering, take the absence of any verification by sense-perception (an absence which, as has been seen, sometimes even emphasized by defenders of that belief) as a sufficient ground for dismissing the belief as based upon illusion. Yet, as I have already observed, the matter is not so simple as it may at first sight appear. The extensive literature dealing with the nature of perception alike from the psychological and from the philosophical point of view sufficiently attests on the one hand the difficulty of deriving our experience of an external world from an experience of inner states of our own, and on the other hand the difficulty of simply identifying the sensible phenomenon with the external object which we commonly suppose ourselves to be perceiving when that is presented to our senses. Thus, even with respect to bodies, the existence of which no one supposes to be known to us except through the senses, the senses *may* deceive, and are *never*, apart from a complementary factor (however we may designate this), the exclusive source of our knowledge of them as external realities. But when, from our knowledge of external things or bodies, we pass to our knowledge of our own or other minds, it is still more clear that what we know is more than we perceive by means of the senses. Probably most people (unless indeed they were consistent Behaviourists—if such there be) would allow this as regards ourselves; while as regards persons other than ourselves, I have elsewhere[1] attempted to show the inadequacy of any view which attempts to base our acquaintance with our fellows as such persons on an analogy between their bodily shape and movements, as perceived by the senses, and our own. As regards the psycho-analysts, however, there would presumably be no need to argue this point; for their fundamental conception of *libido* implies a real relation between persons far too early in its appearance in our lives, and far too essential to our nature to presuppose any kind of inference. Nor can any of those who (like the sociologists of Durkheim's school, whose account of

[1] "Our Knowledge of One Another" (in the *Proceedings of the British Academy*, 1930). Cp. *Divine Personality and Human Life*, pp. 182 f.

religion I have endeavoured to criticize in *Group Theories of Religion and the Individual*[1]) hold that the individual is first conscious of himself as the member of a group consistently deny that there must enter into his awareness of his fellow-members of that group an element other than the perception of their bodies by means of the senses. Even if it be said that *libido* in its primary meaning is itself a kind of sense, it must be allowed that on the one hand it falls short of being *perception*, and, on the other, that—at any rate as it appears in the writings of the psycho-analysts—it is something in human beings much more than a mere sexual susceptibility, and involves such a *rapport* as can only exist between creatures who are not merely animals but, potentially if not actually, persons.

Thus we may say that, on the occasion of certain sense-perceptions, we are made aware of external objects; and on the occasion of a certain group among such sense-perceptions also of other minds; while referring all our sense-experience to ourselves as its subject, we are through it aware of ourselves. In no case is the fact of sense-perception taken by itself the ultimate court of appeal as to the real existence whether of oneself, of another person, or even of an external

[1] Allen & Unwin, 1916.

object; and one therefore certainly cannot take it as the ultimate court of appeal in the case of the existence of God, since God is, according to those most concerned to assert his reality, not an object of sense even in the way in which another person may be said to be such.

This result of our discussion is thus far purely negative, and we have still to see whether there is any positive evidence of God's existence which can be offered to those who deny it on the ground of the absence of any experience of him as an object of the senses, and who support their denial by an account of the manner in which a belief in his existence might have arisen either from illusions of sense or from misinterpreted memories of childhood.

At this point it is important that we should ask ourselves: What is the "idea of God," the belief in the reality of the object whereof certain psychologists are thus ready to explain as arising from some kind of mistake? The assumption seems often to be made that it is no more than the idea of a human person wielding powers beyond those actually possessed by any actually existing human person, but perhaps not beyond those which children are apt to attribute to their parents before the experience of life has convinced them how many things there are that their parents cannot do. But when Descartes, for example, enquires after the origin of the "idea of God" and reaches the conclusion that such an idea could not have entered into the mind of man unless there be in very truth such a Being as is presented to our thoughts in the idea, he is not thinking of an idea which could be traced to a child's vague idea of his parents as able to answer any question and accomplish any task. He has in view the clear and distinct idea of a Being absolutely perfect. Even if it should be alleged that children may regard their father or mother as perfect, he would point out that, granting this, since our parents were not in fact such, we have still to ask for the origin of the *idea*. For we are never content in other cases to explain the presence of an idea in the mind except by pointing out its original in our experience.

I do not intend here to do more than refer in passing to the argument of Descartes which I have mentioned. Students of philosophy will by the mention of it be reminded of a class of arguments, often called "ontological," which seek to establish the reality of an absolute and infinite Being as presupposed by the presence in our minds of a standard by their falling short of which we recognize the other objects of our experience to be relative and finite. The failure of many psychologists to acknowledge the implication of the mind's possession of this standard (which we have, by the way, no reason to suppose that any subhuman mind possesses) is in principle the same defect as has been already noted in their insensibility to the full significance of the capacity of the mind for *knowledge* as removing it from that category of *objects of knowledge* to which belong the subject matters of all those sciences which we call "natural."

It is, I am convinced, natural to the human mind to recognize, in some form or other, beside or rather behind the persons and things which are objects of our everyday experience, the presence of Something or Someone, characterized at once (as I have elsewhere expressed it[1]) by the notes of *ultimacy* and *intimacy*; of Something or Someone in which or in whom is to be sought the meaning of all experience, of ourselves, and of our environment; in other words, of a God. That, at stages of development inferior to that which we have attained, this Something or Someone should be envisaged in ways which to us seem obviously inadequate, even to the point of absurdity, is no more wonderful than that primitive notions of matter and of mind should appear to us fantastic and even self-contradictory. But it is, in the end, as difficult

[1] See above, p. 15, and cp. *Hibbert Journal*, October 1933, "The Nature of Religious Experience."

to account for the universality of the belief in God as for the universality of the belief in an external world, or of the belief in persons other than ourselves, or indeed of the belief in ourselves as persons, otherwise than by the real existence of our own selves, and of the bodies and minds with which we find ourselves continually in interaction, and, no less, of God, in and through their relation to whom we and they are constituted a single world. It is certain that illusions have played a large part in the past history of human intercourse with the external world, with society, and with God; but illusion itself implies some acquaintance with a reality for which we mistake something else; and it is not true that we can, with Freud,[1] simply identify the "religious ideas" of a culture with its illusions, or set down all religion as illusion without at last involving in the same condemnation all other elements of culture, science itself among the rest. I have, in a book to which I have already referred,[2] attempted to show that the "sociological" theory of Durkheim, after denying the objective validity of religion because based upon what he calls "collective representations," finds in the end no other basis for the fundamental conceptions

[1] *The Future of an Illusion*, Eng. tr., p. 29.
[2] *Group Theories of Religion and the Individual.*

of logic and of science in general. Nor have I been able to discover in the writings of Freud and of Jung with which I am acquainted any principle on which a mind, whose religious ideas can be accounted for without remainder as these authors account for them, is nevertheless allowed to possess that capacity for apprehending objective reality, confidence in which is presupposed by the psycho-analytic as by every other theory which is offered by scientific investigators for our acceptance. The only hint of such a principle would seem to be that given by an occasional appeal to verification by sense-experience. Yet (as we have seen) not only are the senses themselves not exempt from liability to illusion, but there are admittedly conclusions, e.g. in mathematics, which no one would deny to be scientific, but which cannot be sensibly verified. And, if it be said that these do not claim for themselves the kind of validity to which such verification would be relevant, we must again recall the fact that in the most highly developed forms of theistic religion God is regarded as not accidentally but essentially invisible, and it is recognized as characteristic of religion in contrast with other spheres of life, that here, as the Christian apostle expresses it, we "walk by faith and not by sight."[1]

[1] 2 Cor. v. 7.

In the remainder of this chapter I propose to comment on the contentions of two outstanding contemporary writers on psychology in favour of the view that the belief in God is based upon illusion. One of these will be Professor Leuba's interpretation of the facts claimed by mystics as evidence of a divine Presence directly experienced by them in certain states of consciousness; the other, Dr. Freud's explanation of the idea of God as a "father-surrogate," the creature of the unconscious wish to recover in mature life the experience of a relationship once enjoyed in childhood.

It is a well-known fact in the history of the philosophy of religion that there has manifested itself in recent times a tendency to base the defence of belief in God upon what is called "religious experience"[1] rather than upon such arguments as formed the staple of an earlier apologetic. These arguments inferred from the adaptation of means to ends discernible in organic life, or in nature generally, the existence of an intelligent Designer; or from the necessity laid upon the human mind of seeking a cause of every fact of

[1] The phrase "religious experience" as now employed owes its present currency in the English-speaking countries to the well-known work of the psychologist and philosopher William James in the *Varieties of Religious Experience*, published in 1902. Cp. the present writer's *Century of Anglican Theology*, etc. (1923), pp. 103 f., and *Religious Thought in England from* 1850 (1933), p. 88.

experience the being of a First Cause; or from our inexpugnable consciousness of moral obligation, that of a Supreme Lawgiver. This is not the place to discuss the validity of these and kindred arguments. I shall content myself with the following remarks upon them. I do not consider that, apart from the sense, mentioned just now as natural to the human mind, of being in the presence of Something at once *ultimate* and *intimate*, the arguments for the existence of God which may be called metaphysical, and which received such drastic treatment at the hands of Kant, could establish the reality of a God who could be the object of religious worship. The consciousness of moral obligation, indeed, does appear to me to lead more directly to belief in such a God. But it does so, in my opinion, only in so far as it involves (as, by the way, it certainly involved for Kant) an emotion of solemn reverence toward the moral law which does not admit of the derivation of that law from any such considerations of social utility as have seemed to not a few thinkers sufficient to justify the behaviour which we regard as morally obligatory. On the other hand, I think it a matter of the highest importance to bear in mind that only so far as any "mystical" sense of presence is the sense of the presence of a Being to whom such attributes are assigned as are assigned to

God in the arguments, "metaphysical" or "moral," to which I have referred, is it relevant to allege it as the sole or principal source of our belief in God.

To criticize Professor Leuba as regardless of this last consideration would be, I think, unfair. In his *Psychology of Religious Mysticism*[1] he does abundant justice to the fact that "whatever" they "may say that seems to subordinate unselfish activity to the passive enjoyment of God," the great Christian mystics have in fact, for the most part, spent themselves without stint in the service of their fellow-men."[2] Holding, as he does, that "the specific qualities of the feelings of rightness and of oughtness are of course undescribable,"[3] and presumably, therefore, indefinable, Professor Leuba finds it easy to suppose that "the universalization of the individual will" is "a tendency generated in man in virtue of his social nature and of the circumstances of social life,"[4] so that the unity established in the individual consciousness of the mystics by their love to the God with whom they imagined themselves to be in communion should pass into a life of devotion to the service of their neighbours. Moreover, since this love to God is, for him, a substitution (most often by people who have been denied, or who have denied themselves, the

[1] 1925. [2] Page 128. [3] Page 133. [4] Page 130.

normal satisfactions of human love) of an imaginary for a real (that is, a human) object of the love-relation, the experience which has given unity to the mystics' individual consciousness is in principle identical with that in which, when that unity has once been attained, they have sought for satisfaction. Professor Leuba fully recognizes that the God with whom the mystics suppose themselves to have to do is not merely an imaginary person, but an imaginary person imagined as ideally righteous and loving. He is also quite alive to the fact that they find in what they take for intercourse with God a satisfaction of what may be called their metaphysical cravings in the disappearance from their consciousness during such communion of any sense of disharmony in the world, and in its replacement by an overwhelming feeling that, not only with themselves but with the universe, all is well. But the circumstance that a feeling of this kind may on occasion result from the inhaling of nitrous oxide, or from certain forms of mental derangement, appears to him to deprive it of all evidential value; and in the last resort he conceives the lack of verification by means of self-perception as fatal to the objective validity of the "sense of presence" which, when associated with such feelings, has been interpreted as a direct experience of God.

It may without hesitation be conceded to Professor Leuba that we cannot find in the mystics' "sense of presence," taken by itself, a sufficient proof of the reality of God. It is true that I believe, as I have already said, that there lies at the root of religion what may be called a natural sense of being in the presence of God; and that, apart from this, the "rational" arguments for the existence of God would have no *religious* significance, whatever their logical cogency. But, on the other hand, it is only in the context of such reasoning as is formulated in these arguments that this "sense of presence," if we may so call it, can be properly called "religious" or its object "God." Nor is it (as Professor Leuba seems at times to recognize) other than exceptionally that it is found in the peculiarly concentrated form which it assumes with certain mystics, where the distinction between the sense of the presence of God and the perception of that of a fellow human being seems to be obliterated. It may even be indeed that this most often or only occurs where there is some abnormality in the psycho-physical constitution, or where the mystics' circumstances do not afford their natural outlets to the sex-instinct or to the "tender emotion." But it must be remembered that *human* love for mate or child or parent in any case transcends the animal instinct on which it is based; and that it is no new discovery of psychologists, but the open and avowed doctrine of religion from of old, that the human love first aroused in the course of the development of the natural instincts within the soul of a being which is not only an animal, but a "rational" animal, finds its ultimately adequate object only in God. That in the history of religion in general, and of mystical religion in particular, illusion has played a large part is not to be denied; nor would it be candid to pretend that this fact does not present a problem, and a very difficult problem, to the theologian. But we may legitimately follow in the steps of Butler by pointing out that the difficulties of religion in this respect are strictly analogous to those of any view which allows meaning or value to the progress of culture or civilization. If, through a psychical process to which illusions are incident, men have at last been brought to a genuine science, wherein a real world is revealed to their intelligence, it is surely not inconceivable that illusions should also occur in the history of the psychical process through which the Being who is *ex hypothesi* the Creator of that real world, and in its relation to whom the mind finds the key to the interpretation of its whole experience, has revealed himself to man. If one has no acquaintance with a person, one cannot mistake another for him; and only they can be victims of an illusion who are capable of apprehending the object which the illusion counterfeits. Even the illusions of the mystics point beyond themselves to a divine reality; nor need all that they report of their experience of that reality be rejected because it is mixed with error. Professor Leuba rejects the report altogether because there is no verification of it to be had by way of sense-perception; and he treats the ordinary Christian's sense of a divine presence (which is, as he allows, quite free from any association with hysteria[1]) as a "moderate mysticism" —implying, unless I misunderstand him, that in the less sober or more extravagant experiences of the great mystics is revealed the true nature of what otherwise might here, in "the rank and file of worshippers of almost every Christian sect," have been uncritically taken at its face-value. I should myself decline to allow that lack of a verification by "sense-perception" derogated from the value of the evidence of a "sense of presence" where the "presence" is confessedly that of a Being "whom no man hath seen nor can see;"[2] while I should regard that sense of being in the presence of God which is, as Professor Leuba admits, shared by "mystics" with multitudes

[1] Page 191.

[2] 1 Tim. vi. 16.

of persons whom nobody would call such, and which is never confounded with the perception of the presence of other human beings, but is very commonly aroused most strongly by the sublimity of nature apart from man,[1] as a more impressive testimony to the truth of Theism than the exceptional lives of the men and women to whom the title of "mystics" would commonly be confined. It is in the light of the common God-consciousness as the chief endowment of human nature that we can rightly appreciate the spiritual adventures of such an one as the "undaunted daughter of desires"; we do less than justice to the common God-consciousness by interpreting it as merely a rudimentary form of what is best understood through the study of these strange and passionate experiences of a solitary soul. It is not to be forgotten how little there is of "mysticism" in the specialized sense of the word to be found in the records of the life of the greatest Figure in the history of religion.

I now pass to the theory, associated with the name of Dr. Freud, which sees in the wish of mature man, who feels himself helpless and insignificant in face of the universe, to find something which may replace the parental protection which his childhood enjoyed, "the father to" the "thought" that there is still for

[1] Cp. Leuba, *Psychological Origin of Religion*, p. 43.

him in that universe an exalted parent who may "exorcise the terrors of nature; reconcile one to the cruelty of fate, and . . . make amends for the sufferings and privations that the communal life of culture has imposed on man"[1] by restraining the indulgence of instinctive desires beyond the limits compatible with social well-being.

The theory may perhaps be described as a specialized form of a more general one which, as Professor Gilbert Murray[2] has expressed it, discovers in "our yearning and almost ineradicable instinctive conviction," "certainly not founded on either reason or observation," for a "Friend behind phenomena," "the groping of a lonely-souled gregarious animal to find its herd or its herd-leader in the great spaces between the stars."

In Freud's version we have, however, not a "herd-leader," but a "father," and a "father" already (it is to be observed) invested in memory with attributes which can never have been really his, but have been imputed to him by the infantile credulity of his offspring. Thus the illusory character which Freud attributes to religion as an imaginary relation to a non-existent religion belongs in fact to that primitive relation to an existing object whereof it is represented

[1] *The Future of an Illusion*, Eng. tr., p. 30.
[2] *The Stoic Philosophy*, pp. 56 f.

as, so to speak, a Brocken spectre projected on the mists of the "mysterious universe."

Now, could we accept the Pauline doctrine that from God, "every fatherhood in heaven and earth is named,"[1] it would be intelligible enough—indeed it is what one would expect—that in the earliest realization of parenthood as the occasion of an emotional relation to the father (though it were in the shape of the "Oedipus complex" which figures so conspicuously in Freudian mythology), the human spirit was already reaching out after a satisfaction of its needs which could eventually be afforded by no earthly father, but by God only. But, as presented by Freud, the whole cultural development of our race is dependent upon an illusion which that same development must at last dispel.

Were there sufficient space at my disposal, it would not be difficult to show that the theory, as put forward by its author, is neither clear nor consistent. But I must content myself with suggesting some criticisms which I cannot fully work out.

I will not dwell upon the admitted difficulty which is indicated by Freud's own confession[2] that he is at a loss to indicate the place which should be assigned in the evolution of religion to "the great maternal

[1] Eph. iii. 15. [2] *Totem and Taboo*, Eng. tr., p. 247.

deities who perhaps everywhere preceded the paternal deities." Nor will I do more than briefly mention here the disconcerting alternation of the conception of the father as a beloved and trusted protector and that of the father as the strict imponent of taboos. No doubt in the experience of many an individual human being a father may, and often does, present both aspects to his children. But where, as is the case on the whole in Freud's account, a racial memory or tradition would seem to have more to do with determining the common attitude which is reflected in the belief in God or gods than a particular individual's recollection of his own parents, it is not at all easy to convince oneself that the primeval father made an equally deep impression on that racial tradition *both* as his children's shield against the assaults of fate and nature and as the jealous tyrant who denied his sons all satisfaction of their sexual appetites. Apart from the doubts here indicated, there is moreover throughout Freud's whole presentation of the matter a strange blending with a license of speculation, which by no means respects the limits of a "positive" and materialistic philosophy, of a dogmatic refusal to allow what is allowed to be "the higher nature of man"[1] any origin other than a retention in the memory of childish error.

[1] See *The Ego and the Id*, Eng. tr., p. 47.

For the "super-ego" which is (so we are told by Freud[1]) the source of the "categorical imperative" of morality, is apparently, in Freud's view, adequately accounted for as the "taking into ourselves" of the qualities we, as children, admired and feared in our parents, who themselves gave us orders which we were compelled to obey.[2] But if these qualities, as we found them existing or supposed them to exist in our parents, were really in any intelligible sense "higher" than other qualities, this is of course no explanation at all; but if they were not, they cannot continue to have for us the value which we then set upon them, except so far as we are content to remain the prey of an illusion. Nor should it be necessary to remind anyone who cares for accuracy in the use of language that an order does not become a "categorical imperative," in the historical sense of that expression, by obtaining compulsory obedience from those to whom it is addressed.

Again we find Freud tracing the "powerful sense of guilt"[3] for which he, like other close observers of human nature, finds himself unable entirely to account by the crimes of which those who exhibit it have been in their own persons actually guilty—in

[1] *The Ego and the Id*, Eng. tr., p. 69.
[2] Ibid., p. 47.
[3] Ibid., p. 76.

other words, what the theologians call "original sin" —to an event the memory of which is, it would seem, preserved in the "mass psyche" or continuous emotional life of the race. This event, which our author strongly inclines to believe historical,[1] and which takes in his system the place occupied in Christian tradition by the eating of the forbidden fruit (an event, by the way, which few educated Christians nowadays would take to be historical), can certainly not (like "man's first disobedience" as related in *Genesis*) be criticized as making too much of a trivial offence. For the sin to which the Freudian "fall of man" is attributed appears to have included various forms of incestuous desire, parricide, and cannibalism. But, though we readily share the feeling of horror with which Freud seems himself to regard this primeval crime, it is difficult to understand how he can not only explain that feeling, but (as he certainly appears to do) endorses and approves it, except upon an assumption of the validity of ethical judgments which is surely quite inconsistent with his whole philosophical position.

Lastly, Freud's express recognition[2] of the legitimacy of enquiry after the "purpose and goal of life," while

[1] See *Totem and Taboo*, Eng. tr., pp. 265–7.
[2] See *The Ego and the Id*, Eng. tr., p. 55.

no doubt an answer to that enquiry may be given without introducing the conception of a "personal" God, yet implies a teleological view of the world which one would have antecedently expected him, on the principles which appear to govern his rejection of all religion as essentially illusion, decisively to repudiate.

What emerges, in my judgment, from a study of Freud's explanation of the origin of the belief in God is a conviction that, while it is in the relation of children to their parents that emotions, both of fear and of love, have been excited and developed, which seem to point beyond their primary objects to one more adequate, the denial that such a more adequate object exists appears to be justified in the end only by the demand for verification by sense-perception as the sole test of reality—a demand which, in dealing with Professor Leuba's theory, we saw reason to regard as illegitimate. On the other hand, the fact that, by the admission of Freud himself and other representatives of psycho-analysis, the whole cultural development of humanity is bound up with what, on their principles, is from first to last mere illusion, puts us into an extremely difficult position. For the existence of that very science, in whose name religion is pronounced to be illusion, assumes a correspondence of the human mind with reality of the kind which in other fields is taken as a matter of course to be merely the "shadow of fulfilled"—or rather of unfulfilled—"desire." No reasonable apologist for religion would underrate the difficulties which faith in God must encounter in the face of the facts revealed to us by the scientific investigation of our own nature and of that of the world in which our lot is cast. But if that faith can claim, as on Freud's own showing it may, to be the supreme expression of that confidence (directed in the first instance toward the human parents) which underlies all science, the confidence that our reason is not an alien in the world wherein it is for ever seeking to find itself at home, but the child of that world's Creator, then those who have embraced this faith will not be deterred by these facts, to which Freud and his followers have directed our attention, from holding to it and yet, while holding to it, profiting by much that these investigators have to tell them of the central importance which (as they had learned before in other terms) belongs to the relation of love between persons as the principal key to the secret of human life.

The resemblance between the declaration in the Gospel[1] that, to enter into the kingdom of heaven, we must become as little children, and the psycho-

[1] Matt. xviii. 3.

analysts' doctrine that religion is essentially the continuation into mature life of an infantile attitude toward our environment, must have struck many. Some would say that the latter gives in scientific language the true significance of the former; that in the former we have an open admission, made without a full comprehension of its implications, of that which the latter expresses in terms that leave no doubt of these. But there are facts, well known to anthropologists, which may set the matter in a different light. I refer to the widespread custom among primitive peoples of initiating a boy on the threshold of physical maturity into his new responsibilities as an adult member of his tribe by ceremonies suggestive of his being *born again*. The disciples of Jesus, if not he himself, symbolized the principle expressed in his saying that we must become as little children in order to enter into the kingdom whose coming it was his mission to proclaim, by making a sacramental "new birth" of water and the Spirit the means of admission into his Church. Here, as in other instances, the Christian religion has taken up into itself an immemorial religious tradition. In later days, it is true, the baptism, which was at first the sequel of personal conversion, and so was administered to adolescents or adults, came to be administered to children newly born; but the "confirmation" (as we say), which had originally accompanied it, was then detached from it and took its place as the rite of initiation into the full exercise of those rights which had been potentially acquired in infancy by baptism. The psycho-analysts have recognized the psychological propriety of this ecclesiastical tradition in their insistence upon what they describe as a second beginning of the sexual life after a pause or period of latency ensuing upon those early manifestations of sexual instinct to which it is characteristic of their school to ascribe so far-reaching an influence upon adult life. We may thus take it as agreed that it belongs to the general tradition of our race to regard as a *second birth* an initiation into that social and spiritual life which is the distinctive mark of the human being. In this second birth the community—tribe, or nation, or church—may be said to replace the natural family; and the grown man is set upon the path of religious development which leads eventually to the consciousness of sharing in a life not to be identified with any finite community, or to be objectified in the shape of a merely tribal or national deity, but only in that of One God, whose will is revealed in the universal obligation of the moral law, and from whose being no form of truth or goodness can be supposed separate. If a childlike confidence is still an element in the faith whereof this God is an object, it is not in accordance with the teaching of history and experience to suppose that the temper encouraged by such faith is normally one of childish shrinking from independence and of timid reliance on divine protection against the terror of nature and the cruelty of fate. Rather has it proved again and again to be capable beyond all other influences of inspiring men with a sense of personal responsibility, with a spirit of self-sacrificing adventure, with heroic courage against fearful odds. Nor is it easy to see how such qualities can really be fostered by a conviction that there is nothing in the real world which acknowledged the demands made upon it by our reason and conscience. Of that conviction what is now called "defeatism" would seem to be the only appropriate expression. Dr. Freud has objected to his critics[1] that they "persist in calling deeply religious a person who confesses to a sense of man's insignificance and unimportance in the face of the universe, although . . . he who goes no further, he who humbly acquiesces in the insignificant part which man plays in the universe is, on the contrary, irreligious in the true sense of the word." I should agree with this remark, if I might omit the word "humbly," and might substitute some word for "universe" which did not imply that faith in the rationality of the world which is the source of

[1] *The Future of an Illusion*, Eng. tr., p. 57.

our conviction of its unity, and which I take to be in origin and principle religious, although all our scientific investigations assume it, and apart from it science itself must wither away. A man who should have wholly divested himself of this faith and of any such sentiment as is suggested by the word "humility," and envisaged his environment as no more than a vast and terrifying welter of things bigger and more powerful than himself or any of his fellows, would doubtless be "irreligious in the true sense of the word." But not so he who, in the midst of his terror, divines a single Reality, constituting our environment a "universe," having that appeal to our moral nature which we call sublimity, and therefore filling us with reverent awe; and who therefore is not merely desperately afraid but "humble" in what he instinctively calls its "presence."

I have already used language which implies that our apprehension of that which lies behind all our experience as *one* and as *divine* is mediated by what psychoanalysts call "projection"; and I have described the highest form of our consciousness of God as a consciousness of sharing in the divine life. This way of speaking may probably remind readers of Dr. Jung of his assertion that "God is *libido*."[1] But

[1] Jung, *Psychology of the Unconscious*, Eng. tr., pp. 71, 120, 227.

neither recognition of the part played by "projection" in our knowledge of God (as in that of our fellow-men), nor acknowledgment of the fact that, in virtue of the vital energy which stirs in us, we "are greater than we know" are inconsistent with allowing that, through and in the living processes which psycho-analysis investigates, there is revealed to us a Reality in which, since we "live and move and have our being" in it, is not the less immanent in us because it is no creature of our own activity, nor even our own activity contemplated as distinct from ourselves, but our *transcendent Creator.*

A distinguished expounder of the "new psychology," after describing "projection" and "rationalization" as "inevitable functions of the human mind which we cannot expect ever to fall into disuse," goes on to compare the mind which exercises these functions to "an Indian juggler" who "can climb up a rope the end of which has been thrown into the heavens."[1] But are we really bound to assume that the functions on which depends all that we most value in life—including, be it remembered, "science" itself—are no more than conjuring tricks—merely because of our submission to the dogma, discredited by the mere existence of mathematical science, that verification by sense-perception is the sole and sufficient criterion of objective reality?

[1] Professor Tansley, *The New Psychology*, pp. 139, 140.

# V

## A VINDICATION OF THEISM

My last Lecture will be devoted to a vindication of Theism against the objections which in the first three sections of this book have been illustrated from three notable works published within the last few years, brought against it by men who are not antagonistic to all *Religion*, but who regard *Theism* as incompatible with a due respect for such spiritual and indeed in a very real sense *religious* values as are revealed in our sense of awe in the presence of the vastness and mystery of the physical universe, or, again, in our consciousness of the obligation laid upon individual human beings to maintain, against all doctrines which would derogate from them, the autonomy of their conscience and the freedom of their self-determination. Thus I shall not attempt such a vindication of *Religion* as may be found, for example, under that title in a remarkable contribution made by one of my predecessors in the Forwood Lectureship, Professor Taylor, of Edinburgh, to the collection of *Essays Catholic and Critical*. Nor do I seek to vindicate even Theism against opponents who do not approach the subject as persons convinced that humanity cannot dispense with what may be called a religious attitude towards life as a whole; an attitude no less remote from mere gratification of "chance desires" and following of momentary impulses, and no less harmonious with reason and stimulative of noble emotion than belief in God has been in the past held to be.

I shall then only endeavour to suggest that, the religious consciousness being taken as a normal feature of human life, the interpretation thereof as a consciousness of the presence of a Being with whom what we may naturally call personal relations are possible, is not only the most obvious interpretation, but also one which there is no necessity laid upon us to reject on either of the two main grounds which we have seen to underlie current criticisms of theistic language and doctrine. On the other hand, I am convinced that neither of the suggested alternatives, a religion of "cosmic emotion," or a religion of what may be called in a general way "humanism"—though this may take more than one form—can so well satisfy as does Theism the actual demands of the religious consciousness in its maturer forms.

From at least the time of Plato, who may justly be called the founder of the classical tradition of philosophical Theism in Europe, there have been discriminated two kinds of "anthropomorphism," the one of which has been by the representatives of that tradition repudiated as heartily as the other has been asserted. This fact is sometimes overlooked, and the term "anthropomorphism" has been, as a matter of fact, commonly associated with the former of these two types of view, to either of which it is possible to apply it. Thus in the history of Christian theology it designates a heresy which prevailed among certain ascetics in Egypt and elsewhere during the fourth century, and according to which there was ascribed to God a body of human shape. The text in Genesis which speaks of man being made in the divine image was taken as giving authoritative sanction to this opinion; the common teaching of the Church, however, interpreted this of the *soul* of man and not of his body.

Plato was no doubt well acquainted with the celebrated attack made by the satirist Xenophanes of Colophon upon the stories told of the Greek gods by Homer and Hesiod, in the course of which he remarked that if lions or oxen or horses were to make images of the gods they would represent them as lions, oxen, or horses respectively, no less than we men represent them as human beings; and indeed agreed with him in holding that the mythology of the poets tended to exercise a pernicious influence alike upon science and upon religion. But he distinguished in human nature a truly godlike element, which we have no ground for supposing the beasts to share with us, namely, the Reason. And indeed, though probably without realizing that it might be regarded as a qualification of his attack upon anthropomorphism, Xenophanes himself, when giving the name of God to the heaven or universe, although he said that this God was "neither in form like unto mortals, nor in thought," yet ascribed to him thought and even sense: "He sees all over, thinks all over, and hears all over"; "without toil he swayeth all things by the thought of his mind." We may say that it is indeed just because Xenophanes' oxen, horses, and lions do not share this thought of *all* things, which we call Reason, that they do not, as a matter of fact, make images of the gods at all. Plato, on the other hand, following in the footsteps of Anaxagoras, and of his own master Socrates, who had welcomed as a new light Anaxagoras' suggestion that the world could not be explained solely as a combination of material elements, but that the unity and order which we find in it implies the presence of mind or reason therein, deliberately affirmed that, not otherwise than our bodies are of the same stuff with the outer physical world from which they come and into which they are resolved, must there be in the universe a Mind from which our minds derive their being, and with which it is homogeneous as our bodies are with the physical world. Plato is, as I said, the founder of the European tradition of philosophical Theism; and it has ever been the principle of that Theism to discriminate in humanity that which belongs to it as an animal species from that in it—the Reason as it has been perhaps most often called—which, being a capacity of apprehending the Whole, the Eternal, Infinite, or Absolute (if only through contrasting with it the other objects of experience as partial, transient, finite, relative) may without absurdity interpret its own nature as akin to that which imparts to reality the unity which we divine it to possess, and makes of it a "whole" or "universe."

Nevertheless, as I have already intimated, the ultimate appeal of Theism is not to arguments, however strong when brought forward in support or defence of a belief natural from the first to the human mind, but to the actual experience of the normal excitation in our souls by the Reality by which we find ourselves confronted and environed, of perceptions and sentiments which, apart from such an object as Theism assigns to them, must be regarded as essentially illusory and incapable of satisfaction. It is indeed, as we have already seen, not to be denied that there may be and are instances of the occurrence of such perceptions and sentiments without the definite envisagement of their object as a Being to whom we stand in a relation analogous to—although not identical with—those which exist between ourselves and other finite persons. But I think that these instances may be accounted for in one of two ways—sometimes in one of them, sometimes in the other. Where there is an inadequate sense of individual personality on the part of any human group (and it seems clear both that this sense is not fully developed in primitive men and that the circumstances of some people have been less favourable to its development than those of others) we find a corresponding vagueness respecting what we may call the personality of the object of the religious consciousness. Where, on the other hand, dissatisfaction has been aroused by current imaginative representations of this Object as transforming to it features of finite personality which are inappropriate to it, there is a tendency, by way of reaction, to deny to it even characteristics which are certified by religious experience itself, and are, in truth, often implicitly assumed by some who expressly repudiate the attribution of them to it.

It is of great importance to bear in mind, in any discussion of Theism, that, if religious experience is, or at any rate seems to be, an experience of Another, in whose presence we stand and towards whom we feel sentiments such as might be felt (though with a difference) toward human persons, and seek to express these in language such as we might address to human persons, yet there is involved in it also a sense of *difference* between That with which we have here to do and our fellow human beings. I suggested in my first Lecture of this course that the two outstanding notes of the experience which we call "religious" might be designated as *ultimacy* and *intimacy*, and that these are always present therein in combination with one another. However we may imagine the object of religious reverence, and although man may and often does imagine it in ways which to a more highly developed intelligence appear ridiculous and grotesque, the image, so far as religious reverence is paid to it, is taken as in some sense standing for that which lies behind ourselves and our environment, and contains, so to say, the secret of existence, access to which may destroy us, or on the contrary give us power over our surroundings, or establish harmony between us and them; in any case, it sets us in the presence of what is *ultimate*. So soon as we suspect what has been the recipient of religious reverence of lacking *ultimacy*, we may continue to fear it and to propitiate it, to love it and to court it; we may even pay it the compliment of calling it "divine"; but it is no longer, properly speaking, our God. The "Quiet above Setebos" of Browning's Caliban may be, like the "high gods" of some savage peoples, thought of as out of reach and above being concerned with us and our affairs; yet the fact that he is "above Setebos" deprives Setebos in Caliban's eyes of genuine godhead. On the other hand, so far as he—or it—is regarded as too far out of reach to affect *intimately* the life or conduct of the island monster, the latter's attitude towards him comes short of being real religion, and he is not in the full sense Caliban's God, though no other can be so beside him. Our fellow-men stand side by side with us over against that one background of all our life, the apprehension of which entitles us to be called *rational* animals; and we are each of us divided from all other human beings by a gulf which no sympathy or love can wholly bridge. Thus they have neither the *ultimacy* nor the *intimacy* which are characteristic of the object of religion—they are not God; and a true Theism is never "anthropomorphic" in the sense of drawing no essential distinction between man and God, of merely making God in the image of man, as it is often supposed to do.

What Spinoza calls God is at once the ultimate Reality or Substance, and immanent in our own minds; and hence the love of this God can be genuinely religious, although no one would apply to the doctrine of Spinoza the title of Theism. Against Spinozism, however, I should defend Theism as affording a justification for the worshipping attitude which is at the very heart of Religion, but which would seem to be impossible for Spinoza, except so far as there survived in his soul a habit more consonant with the religion of his ancestors than with his own philosophy. Again, although worship may, I think, be paid to objects such as Plato's Ideas, the Kantian moral law, Professor Hartmann's eternal values, or "humanity" conceived as the "Great Being" of the Comtist creed, none of these appears, though surpassing in permanence and fulness of significance the individual personality of the worshipper, to have the actual concrete reality which belongs thereto; they fall short of it in this respect, and thus have not the *ultimacy* which belongs to a Being in which, to use the language of the schoolmen, Essence and Existence are one; a Being, who not only *has* but *is* the power, wisdom, goodness which we adore in him. No doubt it is only a *philosophical* theism which employs language of this sort; but the language does but make explicit what is involved in the simplest forms of the religious consciousness, which ever recognizes in its Object not only the most intimate relevance to the worshipper's own personality, but the fullest reality which can be conceived; and it is in our consciousness of self that we have, as it were, the model and standard of reality, of which even the most sublime ideals fall short, so far as, taken in abstraction from an individual being or individual beings who conform to them, they do not have that same sort of actual existence of which we are aware as belonging to ourselves.

Theism then, as I understand it and would defend it as being implied in all true religion, may be described as the express acknowledgment that, if there is in the universe something which always evokes the sentiment of religious reverence, this must, when we think the matter out, possess not in a less but in a greater, nay in an infinitely greater measure than ourselves, that which, recognized in ourselves as concrete individual personality, we are constrained to regard as indubitably real in its own right in a sense wherein nothing else known to us can be. In other words, the *ultimacy* which must be ascribed to the object of religious reverence, the existence of which object is certified to us by the evocation of that sentiment in us, must involve the possession of a concrete fulness of being in no less degree than that in which *persons* possess it. Of the authors who were discussed in my previous Lectures, perhaps Professor Hartmann alone would directly challenge this view on the ground that it is characteristic of the world as we find it that what we *value* most highly in it is ever in range and strength of effectiveness inferior to the soil or matrix whence it springs, which we count of lower worth than it, yet without which it could not come to be or remain in being. This position, as Professor Hartmann is no doubt fully aware, reverses the philosophical tradition, going back to Aristotle, according to which ἐνέργεια or actuality, is always in the last resort prior to δύναμις, or potentiality, and admits that (if the metaphor be allowed) the stream of existence can rise higher than its source. To examine it, would necessitate a discussion of fundamental principles for which there is certainly here no opportunity. But, for my present purpose, it seems sufficient to say that in my judgment such facts of religious experience as are admitted by Professor Hartmann himself, when he speaks of gratitude and reverence as feelings bound up with the outlook on the world of beings conscious, like ourselves, of moral obligation, imply the reality of such a Being as he thinks cannot be supposed to exist compatibly with a clear understanding of the nature of this very moral obligation itself.

Since, however, it is as involved in the *ultimacy* necessarily ascribed to the object of religious experience that we are affirming it to possess what is nowadays usually described as personality, or some mode of being in which this is included, we are quite entitled to do what as a matter of fact religion, even in its most mythological forms, has always done, and refuse to limit the personality attributed to the object of religion by a strict application of the analogy of human personality, which is admittedly not *ultimate* in the sense which I am here giving to the word. Correspondingly, while the *intimacy* which is also required in the object of religious reverence plainly involves a kinship with the subject of this reverence which cannot be possessed by any being less than personal, in the sense given to that word in the last sentence, it involves also something which goes beyond anything found in the mutual intercourse of finite persons, and which is described by philosophical theologians as *immanence*.

God, when religious reflexion has attained to a certain stage of development, cannot be envisaged as standing over against his worshipper as one finite person stands over against another. As the ultimate presupposition at once of ourselves, of our environment, and of the relation between us and it, our personality must be rooted in his, and he, as the poet has it, be "closer to us than breathing and nearer than hands or feet." Theism is not the doctrine of a merely "transcendent" God (it is presumably to indicate this that the word "Deism" is often used in distinction from "Theism" to express such a doctrine); the recognition of divine immanence is as indispensable to a genuine Theism as that of divine transcendence.

It is, I think, extremely important that a philosophical Theism should distinguish carefully between social and religious experience, just because the critics of Theism are so apt to assume that Theism is an undiscriminating transference to the latter of categories belonging only to the former. No recent work published in this country will be found more helpful in this respect than Professor Alexander's *Space, Time and Deity*, although I am unable to accept certain peculiarities of his own theology, and especially his conception of God as a being who, strictly speaking, never is, but is always yet to be. In a Lecture delivered a few years ago before the British Academy[1] I attempted, with the help of this remarkable book, to point out

[1] "Our Knowledge of One Another," *Proceedings of the British Academy*, 1930.

some of the characteristics which distinguish from one another the two kinds of experience to which I have referred. To this Lecture I must refer those who may be interested for a fuller treatment of this subject than I can here give; and will content myself with quoting from it a few sentences which will indicate the kind of conclusions to which I found myself led. "The perception of the external world, itself mediated through sensations from which, nevertheless, taken apart from such perception, merely as feelings of the perceiving individual, I believe it to be impossible to derive our knowledge of external objects extended in space—this perception in its turn mediates to each of us the knowledge of other persons, though, here again, that knowledge cannot, I hold, be derived from the perception apart from a spiritual *rapport* for which the perception itself does not account. But it is not the perception of external objects as such, but only the perception of *certain* objects—human bodies and their movements, sounds recognized as proceeding from human bodies, papers or the like inscribed with marks attributed to human agency and interpreted as signs of human feelings, apprehensions, purposes, or thoughts—it is only the perception of *such* objects that mediates to us our knowledge of other persons. . . . On the other hand, a perceived object may mediate a consciousness of the numinous—to use Otto's word—and here the test of what may be called a social response" (by which we discriminate the perceptions which mediate our knowledge of other persons) "is not usually to be had. Moreover, though not all objects of perception do, nor do any always, mediate this consciousness" of the numinous, "*any objects may* do so, since that of which we are aware in our religious experience is immanent in all reality."[1]

After what has already been said in defence of Theism as an interpretation of religious experience, we may turn to those special criticisms of any such position from the point of view of an ethical doctrine closely akin to the Kantian (though we must bear in mind that Kant himself did not hold his ethics to be inconsistent with Theism) which we found in Professor Hartmann's book. I shall attempt to show that these are not valid; that belief in God is no treason against the majesty of human nature; and that belief in the moral government of the universe does not of necessity involve the denial of man's moral freedom and autonomy.

Leaving to the last the question of finalism, teleology, or, to use a simpler term, purpose, in the world apart from man, a question which undoubtedly

[1] Pp. 15, 16.

presents difficulties, and confining myself for the moment to that of the compatibility of a proper sense of the dignity of man with the recognition of a Being who has created him in his own image, I confess that I feel myself entirely out of sympathy with Professor Hartmann in this matter. I believe that the general verdict of history would be that faith in God, as it exists in the higher forms of theistic religion, so far from encouraging a type of moral character lacking in a proper respect for humanity in our own person or in that of others, has a precisely opposite tendency. A term of reproach which I have already quoted Professor Hartmann as using—"anthropocentric megalomania"—seems to me far more appropriate to the Stoic refusal to recognize any superiority of Zeus to the wise man except that of longer continuance, to Kant's admission that he would feel ashamed to be found alone upon his knees in prayer, or to the kindred sentiments of Professor Hartmann himself, than to the conviction of the Christian that he is the adopted son of God, the temple of God's spirit, and must behave himself accordingly. There have been, no doubt, religions of fear which may bear fruit in an anxious and servile temper and a corresponding practice. But religion has risen above this stage, and it is by the highest in its kind that the possibilities of

K

Religion should be judged; while it is precisely in the ethical monotheism which most strongly emphasizes the belief in a moral Governor of the world, and against which Professor Hartmann's polemic appears to be directed, that as a matter of fact seems especially to cultivate, in those who most seriously profess it, a delicate sense of moral responsibility and respect for one's fellow-men which it would be hard to find equalled elsewhere. Nor is this to be wondered at. For, in such a form of religion that which in our nature is conscious of transcending the finitude and relativity which belongs to it as a natural phenomenon—the capacity to apprehend absolute truth and to recognize an absolute obligation—all, in fact, that we include under the names of reason and conscience—are not regarded as mere unexplained sports occurring in the course of the evolutionary process; they are considered to be, in the traditional phrase, the "image" of the Reality which is manifested in all phenomena, but "reveals" itself in the evocation from the human spirit of the sentiment of *reverence*, which belongs to the essence of all religion and which culminates in the love of God "with all the heart and soul and mind and strength" prescribed by the first of the two great commandments of the Christian Gospel.

It is noticeable that while some critics of Theism

—I think Professor Julian Huxley is of the number—experience a sense of relief when they have made up their mind to reject Theism because they feel that they have shaken off the nightmare of an irresistible tyrant, others—I would instance an able American thinker, Professor G. H. Parker, of Michigan, in his book *The Self and Nature*—find their chief cause of satisfaction in abandoning it in the sense of escape from a "protected world" in which man is "the world's darling, cared for by a benevolent heavenly Father," the conception whereof is (we are told) "too unreal and too little challenging to courage and adventure to keep hold of the twentieth-century man." But this description by Professor Parker of the faith upon which he now looks back without regret is (as I have said elsewhere[1]) in no respect true of historical Christianity. "It may apply fairly well to some moods of sentimental piety which have frequently flourished under the shadow of Christianity, perhaps even to certain theologies of comparatively recent origin which have sprung up about it and drawn sustenance from its roots, but from which a somewhat unheroic optimism and universalism have driven out the sterner elements of its creed. But who could recognize in this picture of a sheltered, timid, unadventurous

[1] *Divine Personality and Human Life*, pp. 115 f.

faith, unbraced by the discipline of real life, the religion of Paul, or Augustine, or Dante, or Luther, or John of the Cross, or Bunyan, or Pascal, or Wesley?"

The other representation of God, as a supernatural tyrant, can indeed show more justification for itself in the history of religion, even of Christian religion; but, as I observed before, it is not dealing fairly with Theism to identify it with a variety of its type which has been transcended. Moroever, it is to be remarked that, whatever may be the shortcomings of a Christian theology which has insisted on the sovereignty of God almost to the exclusion of his love, it cannot be charged with the production of moral characters lacking in a sense of human worth or dignity. On the contrary, there is a real affinity between the ethical temper of the Calvinism which made the sovereignty of God the principal feature of its creed and that of the Stoicism which we may suspect Professor Hartmann of admiring on the whole more than he admires the "humble and meek" disposition which would probably be generally held to be more characteristically Christian. In fact, the belief in divine sovereignty is not in the least inconsistent with a strong sense of the dignity of human nature. On the contrary, even where it is one-sidedly pressed to the detriment of that recognition of divine immanence in the human spirit which is never perhaps wholly absent from a genuine theism, and is unquestionably essential to one which is adequately to interpret our religious experience, it tends to exalt that sense by tracing in the reason and conscience of man the image of his eternal or infinite Creator. In the past the notion has often been common that anyone who denies the existence of God may be justly suspected of a desire to throw off the restraint imposed by a belief in the moral government of the world upon the indulgence of his desires. "Such a suspicion has often been grossly unjust, and nowadays the reaction from the whole attitude which engendered it is so strong in us that we are perhaps more ready to expect in an atheist an austere dignity of conduct than a reckless abandonment to self-indulgence.

"Perhaps even this expectation is rather of yesterday than to-day. It belonged to a generation bred in an atmosphere wherein to deny that there is any God above from whom to expect the due reward of our deeds needed not only the courage to defy public opinion and face public obloquy, but also the strength to maintain a high standard of duty for oneself without the support of faith in supernatural approval and assistance."[1] But it is now perhaps more common to rejoice, with some of those whose writings we

[1] *Divine Personality and Human Life*, p. 114.

have been examining, in the "great emancipation," as one of them calls it, from a belief which is identified in their minds with the unintelligent maintenance of traditional taboos which, under the supposed sanction of supernatural legislation, impede the free development of human nature in all manner of desirable directions.[1]

I now turn to Professor Hartmann's elaborate argument against Theism on the ground of the inconsistency of seeing in the world a "realm of ends" with a just appreciation of the implications of man's moral consciousness.

I think we may divide the case against the world as a "realm of ends" into two parts. In the first place it is said that to *our* pursuit of ends it is requisite that we should be able to count upon strict causal determination in the world wherein we take means toward the accomplishment of our ends. In the second place, it may be contended on Professor Hartmann's principles that, as teleology or the pursuit of ends thus presupposes a causally determined universe, the universe itself cannot be teleologically ordered, as this would be impossible without postulating a further universe causally determined within which the teleological activity of the hypothetical moral governor could take place.

[1] Cp. *Divine Personality and Human Life*, p. 117.

These considerations do not, however, seem on investigation to be as strong as they are represented. When I planned a journey from Oxford to Liverpool in order to deliver these Lectures, I counted no doubt on the causal uniformity of nature at every point; yet my principal dependence was on the time-table of the Great Western Railway, and this is surely determined teleologically by human minds. My journey was not the less purposive that it took place within a system of events which was itself teleologically determined.

We saw that Professor Hartmann, beside his objection to Theism with its teleological view of the world-order as leaving no room for *human* teleology, criticized it also on the ground that it threatened genuine morality with absorption into what its advocates have sometimes called a "higher morality," but which is, in Professor Hartmann's eyes, in fact no morality at all; namely an acquiescence in the divine will as revealed in the causal order, which is thus substituted for the free choice of a course of action as good without regard to the question whether the causal order permits of it being carried to a successful issue or no. As Professor Hartmann himself holds that the course of events, including human actions, is, as a matter of fact, causally determined throughout, the question here at issue between him and theists is this, whether the recognition by man that the course of events which, as initiated by a wrong choice on the part of a human agent, is evil, may nevertheless in the last resort be regarded as good from the point of view of a divine plan of which it forms a part. Professor Hartmann holds that it cannot be so regarded except by giving the lie to our human consciousness of right and wrong. It will be admitted on all hands that the presence of evil in a world ordered by a good God is a problem of the utmost difficulty and perhaps even, as a matter of pure speculation, insoluble. But I venture to think that it is doubtful whether it is really avoided by merely refusing to recognize a purposive divine agency in the world so long as the ultimate Reality of which the world and life are manifestations is still regarded as capable of evoking sentiments of reverence, gratitude, and love which do not deserve to be suppressed (and Professor Hartmann clearly does not think that they do deserve to be suppressed) as merely unjustified and due to error on our part. On the other hand, it is not the case that even such recognition of the comprehension of human wrong-doing within a divine plan as is implied in the famous Christian hymn *O felix culpa quae talem et tantum meriut habere Redemptorem* has, in fact, gone along with a deficient sense of moral issues. It has, on the contrary, been associated with the doctrine that solely through such a genuine repentance on man's part as is possible only where the gravity of sin is fully acknowledged, can that point of view be reached in which a man can himself sincerely adopt the attitude to which the hymn in question gives expression.

It perhaps did not fall within Professor Hartmann's plan, since he is concerned only with the framing of a theory of human conduct, to follow up his argument against the presence in the universe wherein man acts of any teleology or pursuit of ends other than man's, by attacking the possibility of any ultimate teleology on the ground that it would presuppose a universe already causally determined wherein to operate. At any rate, I do not recollect that he develops a contention of this kind, though it would seem to be a natural sequel to his previous discussion. Here again, however, as in the general use of the analogy from social to religious experience, care must be taken not to be its slave, but to follow closely the leading of the religious experience itself rather than general considerations which abstract from the special character of that experience. Man is conscious in his religious experience of a Presence with which he may be in communion as he may be with other finite persons, yet, since the

Presence is experienced as not divided from us by the gulf which exists between finite persons, we can no more bring our communion with God under general rules drawn from our social intercourse with other men—although we must use terms drawn from that intercourse to describe it—than we can, to borrow an illustration I have used elsewhere,[1] "dismiss the reality of the musical experiences denoted by such phrases as thrilling, penetrating, stirring, moving, because the instruments do not get inside our skin, nor their noise shove us out of our seats." "There is a genuine experience which these phrases are used to describe, nor could we as well describe them otherwise; and it we ask how the manipulation of the musical instruments can do these things, the answer would be, 'in the way in which all who are musical know that they do.' In like fashion no one who uses such phrases as 'God in us and we in him' is bound to give any explanation of the way in which the human spirit is included in the divine or the divine present in the human, which shall ignore the *definitely religious* experience."

So in the case before us we may accept the promise given us in the evocation, by the contemplation of

[1] *Problems in the Relations of God and Man*, ed. 1915, p. 251.

life and the universe, of such sentiments of reverence and gratitude as Professor Hartmann allows to be evoked, that, despite all appearances to the contrary, the course of the world is ultimately determined by what we can only call a will for the good; and yet may not feel bound to assume that the operation of that will is subject to the laws which limit the operation of our own. It is no doubt true that we can only direct our activities to our proposed ends because we can count upon the causal regularity of the world which is the sphere of those activities; and thus the system of causal determination appears as that in which any teleological determination of events by us is, to use Professor Hartmann's expression, inserted. But if we attempt to conceive the ultimate nature of that reality which is revealed to us in our spiritual aspirations as well as in our sense-perceptions, in our religion as well as in our science, we shall find on the contrary that, while it is not difficult to see how a causally determined world may be envisaged as a subordinate element which is in the last resort of supreme value (we should not indeed seriously think a capricious fairy-tale world *as* good as what we have, and can acknowledge a high *value* in rigorous determinism) it is far less easy to conceive the emergence of a world of values as, so to say, a mere sport in a universal system of causal determination, whereof no account in terms of goodness and value can be given.

I am not indeed certain that the occurrence of such a miraculous and inexplicable variation, though implied in some philosophies, is in the end all that is really implied in Professor Hartmann's view. For in "the remotest," of which, as we saw, he speaks as the proper object of "love" on our part, I cannot but divine an alias at least of the Platonic Good, if not of the Christian God.

At any rate, I hope to have at least shown some reasons for refusing, in a mood of revulsion from the inevitable crudities of the religious imagination, to eliminate from religion a conception apart from which the religious experience seems to lead to theoretical incoherence and practical frustration; and religious experience, as I pointed out in my first Lecture, thinking men of science are no longer so ready as in a former generation to waive aside as unquestionably making no genuine contribution to our knowledge of reality. It is clear that, in the space at my disposal, it is only possible to hint at the lines which an apology for Theism, as the most satisfactory explanation of that religious experience, might follow; and not even to hint at those on which there might be constructed a more general apology, such as that indicated in the traditional arguments for the existence of God. These indeed I believe that Kant was right in dismissing as inadequate apart from an experience of a more specifically religious kind—such as is, according to his view of it, the experience of moral obligation—to establish the existence of God, if by God we mean the object of religion.

I can imagine, indeed, that my remarks may be criticized from a quite different point of view. It may be said that such a theism as I have been defending is too vague and indefinite to be of any considerable religious value. To this I would reply that I should entirely agree with my critic. But, when in philosophical discussion arguments are directed against the possibility of solipsism or against the subjective idealism which allows to the external world which we perceive no independence of the mind which perceives it, it would surely be unreasonable to disregard them on the ground that "other real persons" is a very poor and abstract description either of human society or "a real physical world" of the mysterious universe explored by natural science. In like manner to contend that a real God is required for the interpretation of our religious experience is not to suggest that religion and theology have not before them an ocean for the exploration of which, as the hymn says, "eternity's too short"; it is only to point out that the ocean in question is not a mere mirage.

# INDEX


Addison, 157
Alexander, S., 142
Anaxagoras, 133
Aristotle, 99, 140
Arnold, M., 39, 78
Arnold, T., 39
Athanasius, 64
Augustine, 46, 148

Blake, 27
Browning, R., 137
Butler, 115

Clifford, W. K., 39 ff., 68
Coit, S., 60
Comte, 9 f., 68, 138
Confucius, 14, 61

Dante, 60, 148
Descartes, 93, 105 f.
Durkheim, E., 103, 108

Emerson, R. W., 66
Epicurus, 24
Eusebius, 23

Freud, S., 92, 98, 108 ff., 117 ff., 127

*Genesis*, 122, 132
Goethe, 54, 78
Grensted, L. W., 5

Hartmann, N., 60, 69 ff., 138, 140, 144 ff., 148 ff.
Heine, 70
Hügel, F. von, 52, 56
Huxley J., 38 ff., 147
Huxley, T. H., 39

James, W., 51, 110
Jesus, 77, 124 f.
*Job*, 65
*John, Gospel of*, 92
*John, Epistle of*, 38
John of the Cross, 148
Jung, C. G., 98 ff., 109, 128

Kant, 17, 25, 34, 36 ff., 44, 69 ff., 76, 80 ff., 85, 111, 138, 144 f., 157

Lampe, 70
Leuba, J. H., 5, 89, 93, 110, 112 ff., 123
Lippmann, W., 60 ff.
Luther, 148

Martineau, J., 74
*Matthew, Gospel of*, 124
Murray, G. G. A., 118

Otto, R., 144

Parker, G. H., 147
Pascal, 22, 30, 148

Paul, 116, 119, 148
Plato, 74, 131 ff., 138, 156
Polycarp, 23
Pratt, J. B., 91
*Psalter*, 35

Selbie, W. B., 5
Shakespeare, 62
Smith, J. A., 23 n.
Socrates, 133
Spinoza, 14, 24 f., 45, 53, 63 f., 138

Tansley, A. G., 129
Taylor, A. E., 130
Teresa, 117
Tennyson, A., 142
Thomas Aquinas, 46

Ward, J., 85
Wesley, 148
Wilson, J. C., 73 f.
Wordsworth, 27

Xenophanes, 132 f.